LOST CITY

The Story of Nan Madol,

BILL S. BALLINGER

OF STONE

the "Atlantis" of the Pacific

SIMON AND SCHUSTER   NEW YORK

Since hardly any photographs of Nan Madol exist, all those in this book—many of them shot from a moving boat—were taken by the author.

PUBLISHED BY SIMON AND SCHUSTER
A DIVISION OF GULF & WESTERN CORPORATION
SIMON & SCHUSTER BUILDING
ROCKEFELLER CENTER
1230 AVENUE OF THE AMERICAS
NEW YORK, NEW YORK 10020

DESIGNED BY ELIZABETH WOLL
MANUFACTURED IN THE UNITED STATES OF AMERICA
1   2   3   4   5   6   7   8   9   10

LIBRARY OF CONGRESS CATALOGING IN PUBLICATION DATA

BALLINGER, WILLIAM SANBORN, DATE.
  LOST CITY OF STONE.

  BIBLIOGRAPHY: P.
  1. NANMATOL, PONAPE ISLAND. I. TITLE.
GN875.P66B34   398.2'34   78–17090
ISBN   0–671–24030–7

TO LUCY . . .
for all her help.

foreword

Everyone loves a good mystery.

The public's curiosity is catered to by the television networks, which supply plenty of adventure-suspense-mystery programs, as well as the great publishing companies that often find their bread and butter in popular "who-dunnit" books. Newspapers, of course, play up a good mystery in banner headlines—and keep them screaming as long as they can.

Unknown to many mystery buffs, there exists today an intriguing natural mystery that has never been solved. A monolithic stone corpse of a dead city, covering about eleven square miles, that died sometime in the distant past at the hands of persons—or for reasons—unknown. No one knows who built it, who killed it, or even why or when it was born. Scientists have nibbled away at the puzzle for nearly a hundred years, but have not found an answer.

Anthropologists, archaeologists, ethnologists, geologists and historians find little common ground for agreement regarding the city. A few areas perhaps, but not many.

And right up front, here, I am not proposing a theory that the mysterious city of Nan Madol was built by ancient astronauts, by visitors from flying saucers, or by the lost tribes of Israel or is the remnant of the sunken continent of Mu. This further excludes all other romantic and semimystical theories that might be dreamed up.

Between us, we will explore a logical theory that I hope to substantiate with sound historical clues. There may be some gaps in what I propose, but none is insurmountable, and perhaps other investigators, better equipped, will take up our search and eventually prove or disprove my theory, or at least come up with a better idea of their own.

A good question to start with: Why should I, the author, rush in where few others have trod? I am not a scientist and hold no advanced academic degrees. Why should I believe that I can find answers where far more distinguished scholars have been unable? I can submit only two explanations, or alibis, in reply. First, I have a driving curiosity. Secondly, I have been a professional writer for nearly fifty years. During these years of writing, I have written many published books, magazine articles and short stories, in addition to hundreds of radio scripts, scores of television scripts, and a number of motion pictures.

In any good story, or each good case, there must be a beginning, a middle and an end.

The beginnings of Nan Madol, for me, started many years ago. I have been reading for a good part of my life, as most writers. There is little profound in the life of a writer; he or she is like a computer. Input is stored, analyzed, and then put out again. Output can be no better than the input. Analyzation is determined by the writer's own background, knowledge, and emotional response. The result is a story. It is also the basic reason why no two writers can ever write the same story in an identical manner.

Many years ago, in my reading, I occasionally came across a short reference to the city of Nan Madol. Interesting, of course; a curio about which little was known. Then, about twenty years ago, purely through chance, I met an old sailor, a beach bum whose name I have forgotten. We were talking about the Pacific when he casually mentioned that he had visited the island of Ponape. My curiosity itched like a chigger bite. Had he ever visited Nan Madol? Oh, yes, he assured me.

Sometime before World War I, when the island was administered by Germany, he had crewed aboard a private yacht that put in there for provisions and water. Over a couple of drinks and lunch, he showed me several very old books containing maps and etchings of the island, as well as half a dozen snapshots he had taken of the mysterious ruins. The photos were yellowed and creased, in black and white, and slightly blurred. He apologized for the pictures and explained that he had shot them from a moving boat ... with a cheap little camera.

I offered to buy the snapshots, but he refused to sell. For an old man, in need of money, his refusal demonstrated the value he placed on them. In a life of traveling the seven seas, his visit to the lost city was a memory beyond price.

My sailor acquaintance has long since died, but I did not forget that out there, a pinpoint of land in the immense reaches of the Pacific, was a tiny island with one of ancient man's greatest engineering triumphs on it.

I continued to read and began the habit of jotting down notes whenever I came across a reference to Nan Madol or discovered new information concerning it. My notes accumulated and grew. Then, several years ago, I wrote a magazine article concerning this most mysterious of all cities. That article led to this book. For well over a year I have concentrated on additional research, haunting libraries and interviewing experts. Late in 1976, I journeyed to the island of Ponape and explored the ruins of Nan Madol myself. Like the old sailor, I will not soon forget the experience.

So, in this book I will tell you what I have found and will attempt to explain the "why, when, where, what and how" of the ancient city. It is a detective trip back into far history. But, because I hope to keep the reading light and enjoyable, I am not using footnotes. Any "facts" that I use can be found among the books listed in the bibliography—if you care to read them. Naturally, when I use a direct quotation, I attribute the quote to the authority making it.

At this time I wish to thank the writers of all the books

whose work made my own digging far easier. I owe them a tremendous debt of gratitude. Also, all errors are my own and not anyone else's.

Clues will be presented as we go along. When the story of Nan Madol is told, perhaps you will reach, and agree with, the theory at which I have arrived.

Or, better yet, you may arrive at one of your own!

BILL S. BALLINGER
Encino, California 1978

chapter

1

In all good mystery stories, the first act of a detective is to visit the scene of the crime and examine the corpse. Let's go to the locale!

The island of Ponape is located in the eastern Caroline archipelago. The Carolines make up the largest archipelago in Micronesia and consist of approximately five hundred islands, which, when put all together add up to a total of 617 square miles. Except for three volcanic islands, all are sandy atolls.

Ponape (pronounced Pohn-pay; the *a* is silent) is of volcanic origin and the largest island in the group. It has an area of slightly over 140 square miles and lies 5,760 miles west and south of Los Angeles, California, at approximately 5 degrees north of the equator.

The main island is roughly circular in shape with a diameter of 13 miles and is almost completely ringed by a reef. Outside the reef at varying slight distances are numerous smaller islands ranging in number from ten to twenty-three—depending on what you decide to call an island. Some are so small as to contain only a tiny stand of mango trees.

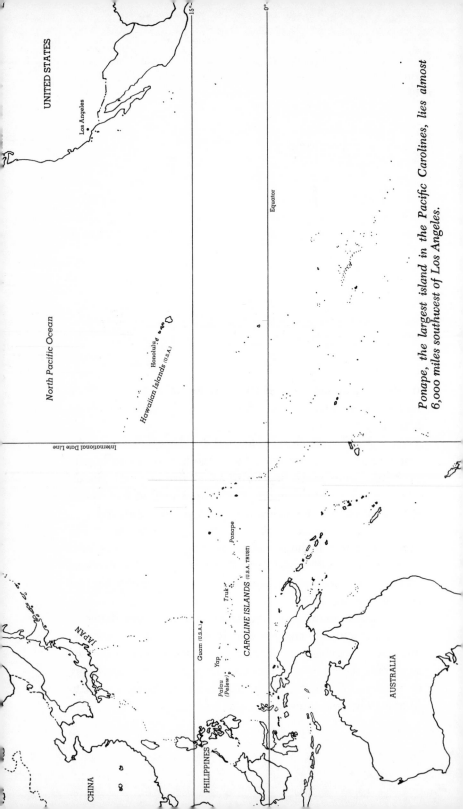

Ponape, the largest island in the Pacific Carolines, lies almost 6,000 miles southwest of Los Angeles.

We will soon square away from these facts and figures, but they are important to impress the awesome isolation and lack of resources behind the mysterious civilization that once existed on this tiny speck of land.

Through the center of Ponape runs a ridge of mountains; the highest is Mt. Tolocome, rising to 2,579 feet wearing a constant wreath of rain clouds. The annual rainfall varies from 185 to 200 inches. Mountains and valleys are thickly wooded; ferns, orchids, creepers, bougainvillea, and hibiscus mingle in a thick underbrush. The center of the island is swampy and almost impossible to travel through. The machete is still a basic tool for most of the island's 18,000-plus inhabitants.

The high rate of rainfall added to the rich volcanic soil means that almost anything will grow—and fast! A Ponapean told me that on occasion the telephone poles actually start to sprout small branches. If this is more than just an interesting story for the amusement of a stranger, then A.T.&T. really has something going for it! The telephone system, incidentally, is for the use of the United States government—the administrator of the Carolines under a Trust Agreement. The administration's main offices are in Ponape, as well as a weather station and an experimental agricultural station. At present, Ponape is also the home of the University of Micronesia with a Micronesian enrollment of 375 students drawn partly from the population of other islands.

Botanical authorities say that floral growth, in some varieties of plants, reaches as much as two feet per day. This gives an idea of how quickly the jungle can take over when left to its own efforts. Man-made structures quickly deteriorate and vanish beneath the hot tropical sun and daily downpours of rain. At any time, the humidity on the island is almost unbelievable. Mildew, rot and decay eventually eliminate all organic traces; nothing survives for very long.

Kolonia, near the northern end of the island, is the capital and only town on Ponape. It has a main street somewhat resembling a movie set of the "Old American West" with touches of Mexican back streets. It is laid out without regard to plan. Most of the structures are one story in height, although an occasional two-story structure may be seen—usually of recent date, made of concrete or metal sidings with metal roofs.

No one seems to have an accurate estimate of the town's population. My guess is somewhere around two thousand persons. Numerous of its island citizens live part time in the town, working occasionally, and come and go as they please. Many of the houses are still made of grass, cane, and bamboo; they are located beneath an overhang of palms with a small garden, a thick tangle of underbrush and a collection of pigs, chickens, dogs and tiny, huge-eyed children. Also in evidence is that good old American curse of the tropics—the tin roof. As an indication of affluence, as well as eliminating a quadrennial replacement of thatching, some Ponapeans flaunt tin roofs on their homes. This makes the houses unbearably hot during the day, but if you think their owners can trot down to a nearby beach for a quick dip, you are wrong. Ponape has *no* beaches. Mangrove swamps grow off the shoreline and out into the water, almost completely encircling the entire island. Ponapeans swim in the rivers and fresh-water lakes.

No paved roads grace the island. Somewhere between 12 and 15 miles of the world's worst dirt roads extend out from Kolonia. Weather conditions make the roads impossible to maintain, although the administration occasionally gives it a try. Chuck holes, potholes and rain-cut gullies decorate every foot in any direction you take. The roads are baked concrete-hard beneath the sun, are flooded daily by the constant gathering clouds, and are immediately rebaked. The holes vary in size from basketballs to large bathtubs. It is necessary, for mere survival, that drivers use both sides of the road, weaving their way in a sort of motor-cross contest with no right of way expected or given.

The United States Trust Territory of the Pacific Islands. Nan Madol, off Ponape, is located in the Ponape District. Nearby is Kusaie, slightly to the south and east. Palau is located to the extreme west in the Palau District. Faraulep is almost due west from Ponape, in the Yap District. (SOURCE: ADAPTED FROM *Handbook on the Trust Territory of the Pacific Islands*)

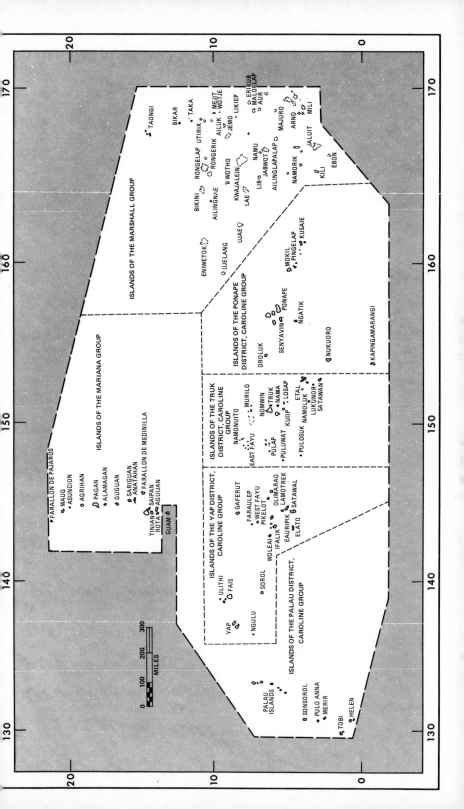

The only bright side to the road situation, which would give the A.A.A. ulcers and heartbreak, are the small children. Immediately after a rain, when the larger potholes are filled with water, the tiny naked children, three to four years of age, use the holes as personal swimming pools.

· The average life of a car on Ponape is about two years. The autos are usually small four-cylinder models originally purchased by Americans or Europeans stationed on the island. At second hand they are bought by the Ponapeans and driven until they disintegrate from rust and neglect. After that, they are reincarnated into other lives. No other form of transportation exists on the island except motorcyles and boats. The cyclists, on Ponapean roads, are a hardy lot. A passenger in a car risks a flattened head as well as a concussion from the car roof. Merely riding a cycle at 30 miles per hour over any road on the island is a calculated risk comparable to Russian roulette.

The boats.

Take your choice. There are all kinds except new. The Micronesians have always lived off the sea; they are good sailors, but not adventuresome or especially skilled navigators as were the Polynesians. The Ponapeans still do a large amount of fishing, but not much from outrigger canoes. A few of the old canoes still remain, but they are used mostly for show or for ceremonial purposes. Modern Ponapeans have home-built inboard or outboard cruisers from 12 to 20 feet long constructed of plywood. They may or may not be built over a salvaged hull from an older German, Japanese or American model. If the motor is an inboard one, you can depend on it that once upon a time it powered an ancient automobile. Regardless of where you sail, you can also depend on the motor overheating, running out of oil, and/or completely breaking down. Usually another passing boat will kindly transport the passengers back to Kolonia.

Smaller, open, launchlike boats are powered by outboard motors. Inside the barrier reef surrounding the island, water is very shallow. In places it may be a foot or less, especially if the tide is out. This poses a problem to a boat with an outboard motor hanging from its stern. The solution, fortunately, is simple: up the outboard and start poling.

The last mode of marine transportation is swimming, an exercise not too popular in certain areas of the off-shore sea, which is reported to be inhabited by sharks. However, the islanders are good swimmers.

One day I chartered a boat for a trip to the ruins of Nan Madol. A boat is the only way you can reach the place. No roads lead to it. The alternative route is over the mountains, through the swamps, hacking your way, stroke by stroke, through the tropical jungle.

The captain of the boat, a young Ponapean, had his cousin as crew. He also brought along his small son, Noah, about five years old. We pulled away from the pier and headed, flat out, at full speed. The old boat slapped and kicked at the water while I clung tenaciously to a gunwale as if bouncing on a trampoline. Meanwhile, Noah climbed over the boat with perfect ease. I became worried that the youngster might be tossed into the sea. The captain remained completely unconcerned, relaxed on a high stool behind the wheel, drinking a can of American soda pop. Apparently, if young Noah should go overboard, there was nothing to worry about. Noah could probably swim like a fish.

It was not that the father did not care about the boy. Micronesians are intensely fond of *all* children, and family groups are closely knit. But to Noah the sea was as much a part of his life as the air he breathed and the island food he ate. All were part of him, and Noah was part of them. So, what *was* there to worry about?

At this point I shall differentiate between the peoples of Oceania. The terms Melanesian, Micronesian, and Polynesian are not interchangeable. They differ ethnically as well as geographically.

In the Pacific, distances are tremendous. The great ocean covers more space than all the land on earth. North to south it is 9,300 miles; east to west it measures 10,300 miles. This is a sufficient area to hold two Atlantic Oceans plus several Mediterranean Seas.

Melanesia means the "Sea of Black Islands" and is in the far-western Pacific. Beginning with the Admiralty Islands to the north, the area extends southeast to the Fiji Islands and includes New Caledonia, the Solomons, and the New Hebrides, as well as parts of Australia and Papua. Melanesians are extremely dark-skinned, often black, with frizzy hair. They are short and of a Negroid type. Some tribes, Negritos, are dwarfish and resemble similar tribes found in Africa. Authorities believe they were the aboriginal settlers in Melanesia.

Micronesia means the "Sea of Small Islands." It is north of Melanesia, just above the equator, and includes four island groups—the Marianas, the Carolines, the Marshalls, and the Gilberts. Most authorities think that Micronesians, originally, were a mixture of Melanesians, and Asiatic migrants plus a proto-Caucasoid type. They are larger than Melanesians, but not as large and physically powerful as the Polynesians. Micronesians are lighter-skinned than Melanesians; perhaps they can be described as dark-brown-skinned, but they are not nearly so light as the Polynesians. Of the three ocean groups, Micronesia is nearest to Asia.

Polynesia means the "Sea of Many Islands." It is a vast triangle, farthest east, stretching closest to the Pacific coast of the Americas. Within this triangle lies Hawaii, Tahiti, Samoa and New Zealand. Farthest east of all is little Easter Island (Rapa Nui) of Kon-Tiki fame. The Polynesians are taller, more powerful, and the lightest-skinned of the three groups. Many have strong Caucasoid features and hair, but with a good amount of Oriental and possibly distant strains of black.

These three peoples have been described in general terms. Exceptions can always be found and argued. However, there is little disagreement among authorities that both the Micronesians and Polynesians are a mixture of races. Undoubtedly at one time in history the three groups came in contact and intermingled to form the basic Micronesian type with which we are mainly concerned. Blood tests have proved a definite difference of blood groups between Micronesian and Polynesian.

The late Dr. Peter Buck, former director of the Bishop Museum in Honolulu, and the leading authority of his time on the lore and customs of Polynesia once said that the ancestors of the Polynesian people probably did live in some part of India. Dr. Kenneth P. Emory, chairman of prehistory at the Bishop Museum, also believes that the early ancestors of the Polynesians might have been proto-Caucasoid.

J. E. Weckler, another authority, in his book *Polynesians: Explorers of the Pacific,* suggests that the Polynesians were a Caucasoid people who lived in early Indonesia until they were forced out by the Malay invasion and eventually found new homelands in the Pacific.

Some, however, go further to claim that the Polynesians were almost pure Caucasian who reached the sea at the Persian Gulf and acquired the art of seamanship from the Phoenicians before they pushed on to Polynesia by way of Sumatra. Other authorities agree as to their Caucasian origins, but point to beginnings in India. Another group attributes origins to southern India and/or China. There is no major agreement.

Certainly the Polynesians of late history were a race composed of various mixtures of Caucasian, Mongol and Negrito descent and may have passed through Micronesia using the many islands as stepping stones from Asia to the far eastern islands of the Pacific.

Some expert anthropologists have propounded a theory that Oceania was the last great world area to be settled; a fairly advanced culture from the *direction* of Asia. This theory includes two distinct streams of migrants, in time, with the last migration around the beginning of the Christian era. As usual, there are dissenters to this theory, and I will explore both sides of the argument later, because they are important to my own ideas.

Nine native languages are spoken in Micronesia, all roughly related to Malayalam, a Dravidian language of southeastern Asia. Ponape has its own Micronesian dialect, which is similar to one spoken on Kusaie, another volcanic island about 300 miles east of Ponape. The two have some common vocabulary and are mutually intelligible. This is unusual in Micronesia, where every island, and sometimes parts of an island, speak such basically dissimilar dialects that they cannot be understood. The islands of Ponape and Kusaie also have another very ancient connection that I can describe more effectively after exploring the ruins of Nan Madol.

PONAPE ISLAND

Ponape Island, showing its
municipal divisions and the
site of Nan Madol. Notice
that a barrier reef encircles
the island, and the shores
(indicated in heavy black)
are an almost impenetrable
barricade of mangrove
swamps.

KOLONIA

SOKEHS
NETT
UH
MADOLENIHMW
BARRIER RE

KITTI
MANGROVE SWAMP
NAN MADOL

0 1 2 3 4
STATUTE MILES

The Ponape District is
composed of nine larger
islands and innumerable
smaller ones. On Kusaie are
ruins similar to Nan Madol.
The Kusaie ruins, however,
are smaller and more crude.
Kapingamarangi is an atoll
445 miles from Ponape and
is, oddly enough, the only
one in Micronesia inhabited
by Polynesians.

PONAPE DISTRICT

12°NN

Oroluk
Pakin
Ant
Ponape
Mokil
Pingelap
Kusaie

Nukuoro

Kapingamarangi

EQUATOR

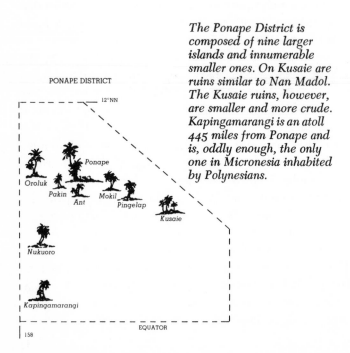

chapter

2

The monolithic stone structures sprawl in gigantic ruins over an area of 175 acres—an enduring monument to man's primitive achievement. Possibly, in the sheer amount and weight of materials moved, and unknown thousands of man-hours of labor, the city of Nan Madol ranks behind only the Great Wall of China and the huge Pyramid of Khufu (Cheops) near Gizeh in Egypt.

Visiting the city is a shocking experience to a traveler. It is hidden from the air and is not visible from land or sea. Nan Madol lies beneath a thick canopy of towering trees and is entirely camouflaged by a thick, interlocking, rapacious undergrowth of jungle brush, bushes, weeds, vines, and moss. The great walls have been wrecked by the thrusting roots of the giant trees, and the cannibalistic appetite of the jungle gnaws away at the skeleton remains without stopping.

As a boat approaches the site, the mangrove trees crowd the shoreline in an impenetrable screen. The only indication of the ruins is the remains of the sea wall, which now barely protrudes above the water in disconnected sections.

Abruptly, as the boat heads in toward the shore, small in-

Nan Madol, from an altitude of 16,000 feet. Behind the straight lines of the old seawall are occasional areas of checkerboard design—the artificial islets of the city. The ruins are completely overgrown with mangrove swamps down to the sea, while a tropical forest and a dense jungle of underbrush make the city invisible from land, sea or air. The extremely dark areas on the photograph are shadows cast by the high clouds. (COURTESY OF THE PACIFIC SCIENTIFIC INFORMATION CENTER, HONOLULU)

A section of the seawall looking inland toward Ponape. Once a great wall encircled Nan Madol; today only a few sections remain. This stretch rises barely two feet above the water.

lets appear at irregular intervals. Later, these are identified as former canals of the great city laid out in a semicheckerboard, elongated plan. The canals are shallow, filled with silt and sand, their banks covered with jungle overgrowth.

If the tide is right, and if the boat draws only a few inches of draft, the craft heads up one of the canals. When the water becomes too shallow, a passenger poles with the crew over the marine debris, or gets out and wades his way through the narrow passages. An eerie silence, broken only by the screams and calls of jungle birds, prevails under the towering green umbrella suddenly engulfing the entire world. Not even the distant insistent pounding of the surf on the reef can be heard.

It seems that little has changed since 1826—only six years after the first missionaries set foot on Hawaii, 3,000 miles east of Ponape—when James O'Connell, a young Irishman, was shipwrecked in Micronesia.

Somehow he managed to reach Ponape, then an island deeply steeped in superstition, intertribal warfare, and cannibalism. The sharp-witted Irishman managed to survive the hostility of the Ponapeans, he wrote years later, by entertaining them with versions of the Irish jig (the Micronesians were great dancers too!) and permitted his white skin to be completely covered with tattoos. The results delighted everyone, except—possibly—O'Connell. But he undoubtedly considered it a small price to pay for an escape from a very personal barbecue.

Ponape was divided into three independent districts (at present it is made up of five) and one of the kings, a Nahnmwarki, offered his daughter, a fourteen-year-old princess, to James for a wife. The Irishman knew a good thing when he saw it and married her. He fathered two sons and remained on Ponape for eleven years. A passing ship, in 1837, offered him a chance to return home. Ever the opportunist, O'Connell accepted the offer and left Ponape for good. Later, he wrote a book about his experiences, containing the first known description of Nan Madol (then referred to as Nan Matol). It is interesting that O'Connell's references to Nan Madol are the first on record, because in 1595 A.D., Pedro Fernandes de Quiros, a Portuguese, was the first white to land on Ponape. De Quiros made no reference to the city of Nan Madol; neither did other Portuguese, Spanish and European explorers who sailed that area, both before and after de Quiros, in the sixteenth century.

After he had learned the language, O'Connell heard the legends of Nan Madol, and decided to visit the ancient ruins on the eastern side of the island. This project probably involved a bit of convincing by O'Connell, because the Ponapeans considered it taboo—a sacred city of the past infested by ghosts and demons. Late as the nineteenth century, they were still terrified of it, and today, many of the older islanders will not visit it.

Evidently O'Connell was persuasive. He talked a Ponapean into taking him to the lost city by canoe. In his book, the Irishman describes his first look at the ruins:

> At the entrance we passed for many yards through two walls, so near each other that, without changing the boat from side to side, we could have touched either of them

with a paddle. They were about 10 feet high, in some places dilapidated, and in others in very good preservation. Over the tops of the walls, coconut trees and occasionally a bread fruit spread their branches, making a deeper and refreshing shade. . . .

In the 150 years since O'Connell's visit, little has changed in the city except that the jungle has taken a still greater toll of the magnificent ruins.

As a footnote to history, O'Connell's experience with his Ponapean hosts was not completely wasted. After his return to Europe, he later visited the United States. He cashed in on his tattoos by traveling in a side show, exhibiting his elaborate skin decorations to the astounded natives of Boston, New York and Philadelphia.

The Cyclopean ruins have often been called the "Venice of the Pacific." The city consists of 11 square miles of buildings erected on rectangular, artificial islets. All construction con-

The monolithic stone walls of the city were built by a cribbing technique—similar to the way American pioneers built log cabins.

sists of basalt-crystal "logs." Basalt is a rock formed by volcanic action. Originally molten lava, if it cools quickly enough it forms prisms and is one of the finest-grained, hardest and heaviest of all rocks. When it is quarried, it can be split into massive columnar splinters resembling four-, five- and six-sided "logs." Those used to build Nan Madol are 3 feet to 12 feet long, occasionally up to 25 feet. The weights may be as heavy as twenty-five tons, but the average is probably around five tons each.

The logs were quarried from a great cliff, 900 feet high, at Sokehs and transported a distance of five to six miles to the city's site just off the small island of Tenwen, which snuggles next to the old principality of Matolenim. The kings of Matolenim were the most powerful on Ponape and resided in Nan Madol. Matolenim is supposed to mean "the space between the houses" and the name "Nan Madol" means "on the stones"—that is, "holy stones," for the city was sacred.

Incidentally, there is a considerable variance in the spelling of Ponapean names. For illustration, the above name of Matolenim may also be spelled Metalanim, Medolenihw, or Madolenihmw.

No one knows exactly how these tremendously heavy stones were transported. The Ponapeans had no knowledge of a wheel, and they had no beasts of burden, so it is probable that the tonnage was floated on great rafts from the quarry to the coral reefs off Tenwen Island.

Estimates have placed the number of man-made islets between ninety and one hundred. Because of the heavy jungle growth and centuries of damage, it is almost impossible to make an accurate count. Each islet was built atop a supporting coral reef in the shallow waters, and projects five to six feet above the surface. All the islets are separated by narrow canals and each stands like a small city block.

The basalt logs were laid down on the reefs, crisscross fashion similar to American log-cabin construction. When an islet was completed, structures were built on it—again using the same type of log cribbing. Gigantic walls were raised, some thirty feet tall or higher, and the spaces between the stone logs filled with smaller stone, chunks of coral, and

28

pebbles. Some walls were over twelve feet thick!

The islets supported monolithic enclosures for the king's palace, a feast hall, administrative center, temples, arsenals, quarters for priests, nobles, servants, forts and tombs. The builders of the city did not use keystones or arches, although they did use a simple slab lintel over doorways, so it is improbable that the stone structures were roofed over with rock slabs or tiles. Experts believe that the inhabitants in Nan Madol built wooden and thatched structures inside the protecting walls. In these they lived and found shelter.

The city is divided into three sections: the lower town, where the king lived together with his court and nobles; the upper town, where the priests resided, and where temples and other religious structures were erected; and the towering, thick outer walls surrounding the entire city and containing tombs, vaults and mausoleums. Commoners were not permitted in the city except on certain occasions; then they had to use separate entrances and exits. Palace servants were exceptions; they lived in separate quarters not far from the palace. A very few stone structures, not on islets, are erected on the shore of Tenwen Island that adjoins the back of the city.

Although typhoons, time and jungle have almost literally destroyed the ancient city, archaeologists have been able to identify some of its more important features.

A magnificent gateway, flanked by two monstrous stones, with massive stone steps, once led to an opening in the wall. This is believed to have been the gate of kings. Two smaller openings are thought to have been entrances for commoners. Among the ancient sites identified are:

Pahnwi. This was built of stone monoliths that differ from the usual basalt "logs." The interior contains two burial vaults from which all bones and artifacts have been removed. Possibly it was excavated in 1896 by F. W. Christian, one of the first Westerners to thoroughly explore the ruins, or by Dr. Paul Hambruch, a German archaeologist, in 1908–1910. The Japanese also made extensive excavations in 1942.

Kariahn. This islet was the official burial site of the priests of Nan Madol. Ketieu plants grow on it—a plant famous for its supposed power to dispel ghosts.

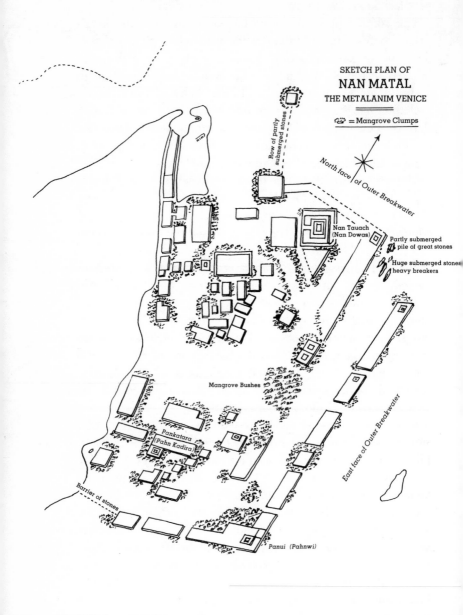

SKETCH PLAN OF
NAN MATAL
THE METALANIM VENICE

⚏ = Mangrove Clumps

Row of partly submerged stones

North face of Outer Breakwater

Nan Tauach (Nan Dowas)

Partly submerged pile of great stones

Huge submerged stones heavy breakers

Mangrove Bushes

East face of Outer Breakwater

Pankatara (Pahn Kadira)

Barrier of stones

Panui (Pahnwi)

A very early ground plan of Nan Madol (using the old spelling of Nan Matal).

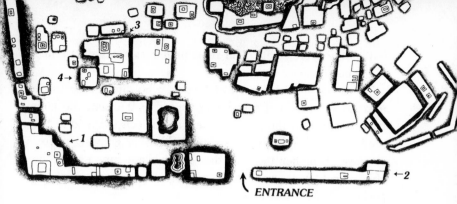

A simplified version of Nan Madol's layout. The entrance is from the sea, at the center bottom. Fishing was centered at Darong (1); coconut oil for personal and ceremonial purposes was produced at Peinering (2); a crude altar was erected to the turtle cult at Pehikapw (3); and the administrative center of the city, Pahn Kadira, occupied twenty acres (4). (COURTESY OF *True* MAGAZINE, BASED ON U.S. TRUST TERRITORY BOOKLET)

Pahn Kadira. The administrative center of the city. The king's residence stood on a high stone platform facing two other stone blocks. Visitors left their weapons on one block, and gifts on the other. This islet also contains a salt-water pool in which to keep fish fresh.

Kelepwel. Just across a channel from Pahn Kadira, maintaining quarters for the servants. What was possibly a playing field for an unidentified game was also located here. Round stones, suitable for throwing in some manner, have been found piled in the court—if, indeed, it was a court.

Pehikapw. An islet containing four pools of water. The names and purposes of two of the pools have not been discovered. The largest pool was used to keep live turtles for religious ceremonies conducted on another islet—Idehd. The second pool, "Peirot" was supposed to have magical properties that could reflect any part of the world back to the gazer.

Idehd. The "Eel Pen." Extremely large, vicious eels used in high religious ceremonies were kept here. Idehd was the religious center of Nan Madol. Once each year, large sea turtles in mystic numbers of four at a time were brought to the island and placed on a turtle shaped rock, possibly an altar. The turtles were baked in special ovens and prescribed parts

31

fed to the sacred eels. The remaining meat was distributed to the people.

The ritual included a special priest who offered the turtle meat to the eels and asked forgiveness for himself, the king (Saudeleur) and the people. The way the eels snapped at the proffered food indicated their withholding or granting of forgiveness. Whether the eels themselves were supposed to be able to call down vengeance or were representatives of superior gods I do not know.

In 1963, a Smithsonian expedition carbon-dated accumulated material and fire remains from the turtle ovens to set a date of 1285 A.D., plus or minus fifty years. More of this later.

Darong. A small stone-walled lake on this islet has a tunnel

This is possibly one of the first plans drawn of Nan Dowas, the monolithic stone fortress-temple-tomb of the ancient Saudeleurs, rulers of Nan Madol. The structure nearly covers the artificial islets on which it is built. The area in the center is where the most ancient tomb is located. The top of the tomb is covered over with huge basalt-crystal logs weighing from five to fifteen tons each. (DRAWING BY F. W. CHRISTIAN, FROM HIS BOOK *The Caroline Islands*)

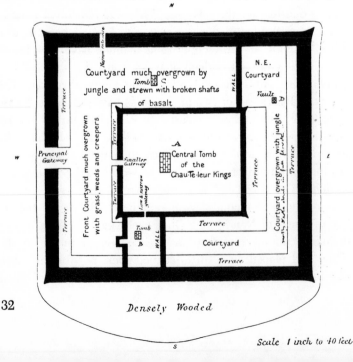

The second of three massive walls (at this point 12–15 feet high—
about half of their original height) enclosing Nan Dowas. The
entrance leads into the ceremonial complex. Commoners were
never permitted to use this entrance under pain of death.

Through this opening in the third wall is the interior of the temple
complex. The arrow points to the top of the royal tomb, barely
visible, in the courtyard.

The small dark opening leads into the royal tomb. The opening is barely large enough to pass a body through. At one time, a large boulder may have blocked the entrance.

extending from the bottom of the center of the lake to a point outside the reef. The tunnel permits fish and clams to enter the lake with rising tides. It might also have been used as an escape tunnel for messengers and scouts in times of siege. Obviously, a very powerful swimmer would be required, but at low tide possibly the roof section of the tunnel might not have filled to the ceiling and could contain small pockets of air.

Today the tunnel is almost completely obstructed with debris and is difficult to explore.

Pehi en Kitel. This is the only islet connected to Tenwen Island. Many ancient tombs are located on it, some—supposedly—of the old Saudeleurs and Nahnmwarkis.

A Japanese excavation in 1928, when Japan still had a mandate over the Carolines following World War I, is reported to have dug up ancient bones here; bones *far larger* than the normal Ponapean scale.

Peinering. You might call this islet a "manufacturing center." It served as a supply and production facility to yield quantities of coconut oil necessary for cooking, medicine, and lamp fuel. Equally important, coconut oil was used to oil the inhabitants' bodies to protect the wearers both from evil spirits and from enemies—physically as well as magically.

Pehikapw Sapwawas. Apparently, loudspeakers and broadcasts are not new innovations. An official herald was stationed on this islet. Standing on the largest rock, in a special four-rock formation, he shouted royal proclamations aloud. The broadcast announcements were repeated by drums over farther distances.

Konderek. A large feast house was located on this islet. Here final ceremonies for the dead were held with *sakau*-drinking and dancing. Sakau is an official ceremonial drink, still popular, similar to kava found among other Oceanic groups. It is made from plant roots and is mildly narcotic. Having attended a ceremonial drinking of sakau (pronounced "sohw-koo") on Ponape, I can testify that it tastes absolutely terrible.

Nan Dowas. Nan Dowas is the most famous and best preserved of the remaining structures in Nan Madol. Located near the main entrance to the city, this Cyclopean structure

These huge stone logs lie over the top of the royal tomb. Only a few bones have been found here and no artifacts have ever been recovered. If the inhabitants of Nan Madol buried personal belongings with the dead—and it is not certain that they did—the high humidity would cause quick deterioration and decay. It is also possible that early discoverers looted the relics. However, it is almost certain that "treasure" in the Western sense never existed here.

was used only in times of war. Although it is a strong fortress, with the top stones of the walls overhanging to make scaling difficult, Nan Dowas also served as a high temple. In the center of the construction is a shallow tomb for royal burials. Behind the outer walls, to the rear, a deep narrow dungeon held war prisoners and criminals.

Two islets, *Dowas Powe* and *Dowas Pah,* on either side of Nan Dowas were garrisoned with guards under the command of a general carrying the title of "Sawpohndowas."

The nobility, *Soupeidi,* entered through the main gates of this fortress-temple, but commoners were forced to use two low tunnels through the walls.

Many other islets in the city remain to be identified and explained. The unbelievable jungle growth covering the ruins, the ages of deterioration, the lack of any written history regarding it, and the absence of human remains and artifacts, make identification and accurate explanation difficult, if not impossible.

Nan Madol is a prehistoric and primitive city in the most primal sense. The great prisms with which it was built were loosely fitted, but never worked and finished for close joining, although oddly enough, the canals were lined with fitted stones. The builders did not use mortar or cementing materials of any kind. No stone carvings or reliefs decorate any of the buildings, and no idols or statues have ever been found. As pointed out earlier, the Nan Madol engineers seemingly had no idea of true or false arches; neither did they use buttresses.

It has long been believed by many authorities that Nan Madol was built by a seafaring people. Certainly everything about the city is sea-oriented.

A United States Department of Interior report states that thousands of man-hours of organized and well-directed labor were required to quarry, transport, and build the man-made islands and structures that cover the 11 square miles. This same report goes on to state: "The unwritten history of Ponape indicates that Nan Madol was constructed by or under the direction of people not native to the Island of Ponape."

Who then, we might well wonder, did build it?

chapter

3

One of the first mysteries to try to solve is *when* Nan Madol was built—or at least approximately when the building of the city began. It is possible, even probable, that its construction covered a long period of time—as much as a century or more.

I have noted earlier that the European explorers of Oceania, in the sixteenth century, gave no reports of the ancient city on Ponape. Possibly there are several reasons for this: the ships sailed around the island, outside the reef, and as I have described, the old ruins are invisible on the shore. When the sailors made contact with the Ponapeans, mutual lack of knowledge of the other's language caused a complete breakdown in communications and information was not exchanged. Or, a third possibility is that the Ponapeans simply did not refer to their sacred city which was long dead and already buried in the mists of legend.

It was not until the nineteenth century, when missionaries and whalers visited the island in large numbers, that general knowledge regarding the city became available. James O'Connell filed the first report.

Some authorities agree that the city was not built by the present race of Ponapeans. Others, however, violently disagree regarding its great age and assert that Nan Madol was constructed not earlier than a few centuries before the beginning of the nineteenth century. This would place a date around the beginning of the seventeenth century or a little earlier. But we have already seen that there was no evidence of it reported by the sixteenth-century explorers, and in the nineteenth century—in 1826 to be specific—O'Connell reported it as very ancient ruins. It is doubtful that Nan Madol could have been erected, been deserted, and gone to ruin in the two hundred years or so between the late 1500s and early 1800s. Certainly, it is hard to explain how all memories of its construction have been lost to the inhabitants of Ponape and, whatever its true history, turned into myths and legends in such a short time.

In Polynesia, as an example, a generation is reckoned as twenty-five years. Some royal lines have tribal genealogies, committed to memory, going back twenty-five to twenty-eight generations. This covers a time span of up to seven hundred years. A chief in New Zealand, appearing in the Maori Land Court, took three days and included ancestors who lived eight hundred years earlier and more than 1,400 names. It is difficult to believe that the Ponapeans could lose all memory of such an engineering feat in a mere eight or ten generations. It is true that they have legends concerning the city; these are mostly unsatisfactory, as you will see.

It has been said that great cultures rise and fall, but they rarely disappear without leaving at least some inheritable impression among the surrounding peoples or directly on their own local successors. This is not necessarily true. The great Hittite empire disappeared from history without trace for several thousand years. Until rediscovered in 1906, by Hugo Winckler, a German scientist, it was known only through references in the Bible and other ancient historical writings.

Micronesian legends say that Nan Madol was built by a black race. This is supported by Ponapean legends regarding a black dwarfish race who lived in the mountains of the island. Skulls found beneath ruins of Nan Madol have also indicated Negroid characteristics. These are not the same *large* bones found on Pehi en Kitel.

Stone barricades and walls are not unknown elsewhere in Micronesia, but they are nothing like the huge stone construction of the planned city of Nan Madol. The only similar construction is on the island of Kusaie, south and east of Ponape. This site, named In-Sa-Re, is not so large as Nan Madol, and is even more rough and primitive in execution. It is not improbable that Kusaie may have been an outlying settlement of the Nan Madol maritime empire, if one existed.

Of the huge, natural basalt prisms used in the towering walls of Nan Madol, some are larger than the blocks used in the pyramids. No tools were used on the stones in Nan Madol. The igneous rock is too hard to work by primitive tools. The Ponape islanders possessed no metal tools and probably owned only axes of Tridacna, a sea shell, too brittle to work the hard stone.

Carbon-14 dating has indicated 700–800 A.D. as the time of the first settlement of Hawaii—three thousand miles east of Ponape—by the Polynesians, who are believed to have come through Micronesia on their way east. Some archaeologists say that Nan Madol was built around 900 A.D., but others maintain the old city goes back to before the beginning of the Christian era, two thousand years or more.

Although the Polynesians have built elaborate, raised stone dance platforms, fitted stone walls, and very low-stepped pyramids for ceremonial purposes, they never built a stone town or village. Their largest constructions, too, have been of fairly recent date. The Polynesians, like the Micronesians, were a stone-age people. They used shell, wood, bone and stone for tools and weapons. They knew no form of metal, although a very few small deposits of iron ore are present in certain Polynesian areas. In addition, neither the Polynesians nor the Micronesians used or made pottery. Some very ancient shards of pottery and rusted iron artifacts have been found in Melanesia, which we will get back to later.

The Polynesians and Micronesians had no need of pottery. Coconut shells and gourds filled their requirements for liquid containers and were easily available. Furthermore, good pottery clay is not found in either of these two areas. If the early migrants through the western and eastern seas had ever known the art of pottery making, it was soon forgotten and lost through lack of necessity. This lack of pottery is pointed out because shards are important to archaeologists for accurate dating purposes.

Nan Madol commanded a rude agricultural system. As mentioned earlier, anything grows. Sago palms, bananas, mangos, oranges, limes, ginger, yams and taro were present in abundance. As a society, it lacked writing, all fine arts, other and supporting cities, and niceties of civilization. Yet it was able to tower above all the other societies surrounding it.

No one knows what the population of Nan Madol might have been at its height of power, or the total number of islanders on Ponape. American ships first reached Micronesia in 1791 and began to chart the islands and archipelago. In the 1850s and '60s, whalers were frequent visitors to Ponape and Kusaie. In 1800, the ships brought Western diseases aboard, which reduced the then population of 15,000 Ponapeans to fewer than 3,000 in the 1850s.

Originally the island was divided into three autonomous municipalities, each under the rule of a king. Later, under European occupation, two more divisions were added. The five: Sokehi, Kiti, Net, U, and Matolenim. Of all the rulers, the Nahnmwarki of Matolenim was the most powerful and commanded the highest respect. The top Ponapean chief of each division carried the title of Nahnmwarki, which was received through two lines of nobility or, in some instances, achievement.

Dr. Paul Hambruch, of the Ethnological Museum, Hamburg, Germany, in 1908–1910, first surveyed the site of Nan Madol and its separate buildings to provide an explanation of their various functions. Since that time additional information has been added and some changes made to Dr. Hambruch's explanations and maps.

Sensational reports have long circulated around the ancient city. Some writers have claimed that priceless artifacts, bones, and treasures have been discovered and removed by the early excavators. *What* missing artifacts and bones have never been specified. Gold, precious metals, and jewels were unknown in ancient Oceania. Pearls and jade are the exception, and they are not jewel stones. Nan Madol may well have been a seaport and, through its marine empire, have traded widely, but I doubt that it ever ranged far enough to accumulate gold, silver and precious stones.

Stone knives, and other stone or shell artifacts, bones and charcoal are about the only treasures found in Nan Madol. The humid, tropical, jungle conditions are responsible for very few of these ever being found, not thieves!

Thor Heyerdahl, scientist and famous explorer of Easter Island, proposes a theory that Polynesia was discovered and colonized from the Pacific shores of Peru by South American seafarers who sailed *westward*. He offers evidence to support his theory by citing the favorable ocean currents and prevailing winds making voyages possible and subsequently the cultural traits held in common by the Indians and Polynesians. He also reports that the Spanish Mendaña expedition, which first discovered the Marquesas in 1595, was given explicit sailing directions by the Incas of Peru.

On the other hand, equally respected ethnologists and archaeologists strongly oppose Heyerdahl's theory and support another: the aboriginal inhabitants of Melanesia and Micronesia were black and had been established in those areas for thousands of years, immigrating from Indonesia after originally leaving Asia. This group of scientists believes that, after the blacks, the first settlers in Micronesia were Caucasian-featured Polynesians. Many of the islands they landed on were so poor in natural resources that, later, great numbers sailed on eastward to Tahiti and Samoa. Meanwhile, they were forced to give up many of their skills. Those remaining in Micronesia intermarried with later waves of migrations, some from Asia, which accounts for the Micronesian's oriental characteristics. According to this theory, the Marquesas were the last group of islands to be settled. But, again, the Marquesas were already occupied by a still older group of settlers when the Polynesians arrived.

Discussions and arguments regarding these two so different theories continue.

As one digs around attempting to find clues to the mystery of Nan Madol, one must remember that history depends on writing. A preliterate society has no true history. Instead, it has a body of myths, timeless, undated and often fantastic, which *might* contain an occasional fact preserved like a fly in a piece of amber. In time even these few facts become distorted and practically useless for preserving the past of the tribe. Orally transmitted memory of important events may be fairly accurate going back for perhaps several centuries, but not much further. Some experts even claim that 150 years is about the limit, but this may be too short. Generally, however, word-of-mouth records will not go on forever and will be lost eventually in later events.

Neither the Micronesians nor the Polynesians possessed writing, and the Polynesians made special effort to memorize genealogies, as did the Micronesians to a lesser extent. This is not enough.

Some anthropologists are of the opinion that primitive people cannot make up their own myths because they (the tribe) hold strictly to reactions of their own senses and receive no new ideas from outside sources, holding only to the familiar things in their lives.

Other experts violently disagree. This school of thought maintains that "savages" are like other people—some smart, some stupid, and that the more brilliant ones do contribute to the tribal culture with new elements.

The fact is, however, that myths and legends often do have some basis in fact, but the fact may be so small and confused that it is impossible to reconstruct history from it. It is impossible to discriminate fancy from reality without a solid stock of evidence.

At the least, Nan Madol was constructed hundreds of years ago; it might well be thousands. The history of its famous ruins remains a mixture of fact, fiction, researchers' theories, and Ponapean legend.

chapter

4

Legends, myths and folklore are not the same. A distinction exists between them, although it is often difficult to distinguish:

A legend may or may not be based on historical events.

A myth is a traditional story, accepted as historical, containing beliefs of a people concerning the creation, gods, universe, life and death, et cetera.

Folklore consists of a people's unrecorded traditions as they appear in its culture, beliefs, magic and ritual.

All three are attempts to make mysteries understandable and even justifiable. To primitive minds, such natural events as an eclipse, must be explained; as they have no scientific explanation, the phenomenon is attributed to a supernatural power—gods, demons and magic.

The detectives I am using to try to solve the mystery of Nan Madol are not infallible private eyes of popular fiction, but are anthropologists, archaeologists, paleontologists, geologists, historians and ethnologists. As I go along it will be found that some authorities' interpretations are credible, some are incredible, but it should be agreed that any reasonable hypothesis is defensible. This does not mean that I shall defend a far-out thesis as simply more than what some people believe, and as a temporary aid to my deductions.

The quest is exciting. Bits and pieces of clues may have started before historical times. New clues have been added in each following age and passed on to modern times. It is up to me to evaluate them and draw my own conclusions. Possibly, some of the answers are in my own mind. That does not prevent me from developing alternate hypotheses and expanding them to test facts relative and important to my own questions. As an amateur, however, I am not an expert and must guard against wishful thinking and sensational fantasy. Self-honesty is important.

The people of Ponape have no collective memory of when the great city of Nan Madol was built—and no written history exists concerning it. The project, probably, was too large for the Ponapeans to handle alone, so other workers from neighboring islands may have been called in to help. Again, from the outsiders, there is little explanation, and it is very similar to the Ponapean interpretation. The outer islands' version goes like this: In the beginning the tribes of Ponape had no names. The people were not enlightened and had no faith or religion. No rites, rituals or ceremonies existed from earlier times.

Two young men lived in Sokeh, on Ponape; their names were Sipe and Saupa. The ignorance of their fellow islanders concerned them so greatly that the two youths decided to build shrines and begin holy rites. They started to build shrines on Ponape and continued until a number of them had been erected. But for one reason or another, the two were dissatisfied with each shrine they had erected. Finally they built fifty structures in "Madolenihmw."

Both Sipe and Saupa were great magicians. They were able to call the stones in such a way that the gigantic basalt logs came of themselves to make up the huge buildings.

The Ponapean version differs slightly. The island of Ponape had a very large population, but no form of government and no traditional leader or ruler. One day two young men arrived on the island in a large canoe. No one knows whence they came. The two men were brothers—Olsihpa and Olsohpa. The brothers quickly became leaders and agreed to build a place of worship outside Sokeh. They built a structure to be used as a temple and also as a seat of government. However, the work on the *pehi* ("stone structure") was not satisfactory, as it was too exposed to the sea. The site was moved eastward to the shore of Net Mountain, and later, again, to Nankopworemen, in U, for the same reason. Remains of these rock ruins are still there today.

Eventually, they built Nan Madol. Again, great magical powers were attributed to the two brothers, who, through incantations, forced the heavy stone logs to fly through the air to exact positions in the buildings on Nan Madol. The city was built in one day.

The two brothers ruled the island together until Olsihpa died. The surviving brother, Olsohpa, became the first Saudeleur (Lord of Deleur). He established a succession of sixteen Saudeleurs with absolute power over all of Ponape. These rulers are remembered only through legends and folklore. The dates of their reigns are uncertain. Twelve generations of Saudeleurs ruled in peace; the Ponapean people became soft and their military arts forgotten. Therefore, the island fell easy prey to the ancestors of the modern Ponapeans who came from the south under a warrior chief—Isokelekel.

The last Saudeleur was Saudemwohl and he was overthrown by Isokelekel, who established a new line of rulers—the Nahnmwarkis. Up to modern times, twenty-one Nahnmwarkis have reigned over Ponape.

According to legend, Isokelekel and his invaders came from the island of Kusaie. This is the smaller island I have noted before, containing the ruins of In-Sa-Re, similar to, but cruder than, the ones on Ponape.

Supposedly the reigning Saudeleurs numbered sixteen. However, not all of them can be identified and it is impossible to establish even tenative dates for their reigns. If Olsohpa was the first Saudeleur of the dynasty, and Saudemwohl the last who was killed in battle by the invader, Isokelekel, fourteen remaining Saudeleurs fill out the royal list. Only half, seven in all, are reported through legends and folklore:

Mwohn Mwei was the first Saudeleur to succeed after Olsohpa.

Inenen Mwei firmly established a respected aristocracy within the Ponapean society. His reign has been called "a very good" one.

Sakone Mwei. If Inenen Mwei's reign was a very good one, then this one is "the period of cruelty." Sakone Mwei raised taxes and ruthlessly collected them. By death, if necessary.

Raipwenlang is another skilled magician.

Saraiden Sapw supposedly accumulated great wealth. He established the custom of the Saudeleurs collecting the first fruits from all the entire island. This is reminiscent of the practice of seignorial rights in medieval Europe.

Raipwenlake, a notorious monarch. Through occult powers he was able to locate the fattest Ponapeans. These were further fattened, and he dined on them with great pleasure.

Ketiparelong's wife committed suicide. She was a glutton for liver; the suffering people served her a portion of her own father's liver to satisfy her greed. Upon discovery of the true nature of the delicacy served at her banquet, the queen took her own life. So did the king when he heard she was dead.

Another Saudeleur, whose name is unidentified, is remembered for having a wife whose mother was a crocodile. Husband, wife and mother-in-law all died in flames when the Saudeleur set fire to his mother-in-law's house.

Often the names and attributes of the Saudeleurs became confused. For example, Raipwenlang is sometimes reported to have accumulated great wealth; it is Saraiden Sapw who was the skilled magician, et cetera. Other than the first Saudeleur, his successor, and the last of the line, there is no accurate order in which the Saudeleurs appeared. Nor do we know the lengths of their reigns.

It is an axiom in history that late-comers have a way of effacing the traces of their predecessors.

The later conqueror of Nan Madol, Isokelekel, established the line of Nahnmwarkis—rulers of both the island and the city. The date of Isokelekel's invasion is also undetermined. Following Isokelekel's rule were:

Luhk en Mwei Maur who was Isokelekel's nephew. Luhk en Mwei Maur introduced a new title of "Nahnlken" for the opposite line of rule.

Nahluhk Nahnsapwe. Nothing known about him.

Nahluhk en Sounpwong. Ditto.

Nahluhk en Nahr. Again, ditto.

Luhk en Mallada may have been the last Nahnmwarki to live and rule in Nan Madol.

Luhk en Peidoh. No details known concerning him.

Luhk en Wisenday. Another blank.

Luhk en Weid murdered his son.

Luhk en Ned had thirty wives.

Luhk en Nen. Nothing known about him.

Luhk en Mwer, although sickly and with a weak body, carried on many wars.

Luhk en Kesik is the first ruler to whom an accurate date can be attached. Luhk en Kesik was responsible for the massacre of the crew of the *Falcon,* a British ship. In 1836, two British warships, the *Unity* and the *Lambton,* avenged the deaths of their countrymen. Luhk en Kesik was shot, and his brother was captured and hanged as an example.

Luhk en Kidu, a British sympathizer, was appointed Nahnmwarki by pressure from Westerners. He ruled until 1854, when a terrible smallpox epidemic almost wiped out the population of the island. Luhk en Kidu was one of the casualties of the disease.

Luhk en Mwei was undistinguished. He ruled from 1854 to 1855.

Nahnmwarki ———? He remains unnamed because he made his son the Nahnmwarki of Madolenihmw, when the son was not a rightful heir. Tradition required the son to be born during his father's rule.

Nahnmwarki Paul, ruling from 1872 to 1896, for a while held the dubious distinction of shooting all Christians on sight! Eventually, he was converted to Christianity and became the first Christian Nahnmwarki. As reported of many converted sinners, he developed into a devout man.

Nahnmwarki Hezikiah, reigned 1896–1898, had three wives and entertained them with the many songs he had learned. History does not report the titles of the songs, which evidently kept his wives happy. (A sore loss!) He also gave missionaries land for their missions.

Nahnmwarki Soloman simply ruled from 1898 to 1928, without much distinction except to evade trouble.

Nahnmwarki Alexander's reign was very short—1928–1931.

Nahnmwarki Moses Hadley was a great-grandson of Jim Hadley, an American, who arrived on Ponape via a whaler. This Nahnmwarki held the longest reign of all—thirty-five years, from 1931 to 1966.

Nahnmwarki Samuel Hadley was the last Nahnmwarki to assume the title, in 1966.

This list of Nahnmwarkis presumably begins immediately after the death of Isokelekel, but it is not certain. Not until recent times have we a definite chronological order. As with the Saudeleurs, especially in the more distant past, attributes of the rulers become confused and sometimes are assigned to one Nahnmwarki or to another. Authorities disagree because there is no way to check the king lists against historical events such as was done to establish quite accurate dates and reigns of the ancient Pharaohs of Egypt.

After reading what is remembered about the Saudeleurs and the Nahnmwarkis, a reader is impressed by the banality and barbaric fantasy assigned to the Saudeleurs. So, too, the early Nahnmwarkis. It is difficult to believe that these rulers could have organized and carried through the tremendous building job required to erect Nan Madol!

Ashley Montagu, reknowned anthropologist, has said, "The criteria by which a culture may be recognized are (1) that it must be invented; (2) that it must be transmitted from generation to generation; (3) that it must be perpetuated in its original or in modified form."

At some time in the past, Nan Madol appears to be the ultimate achievement of a society and civilization that disappeared behind a curtain of time. Certainly neither the city nor the island supporting it meets any of the criteria required by Dr. Montagu. The primitive construction of the city is unique in the areas of Oceania, but not, necessarily, elsewhere in the world. If it were "invented," then the invention rests in the ancient Mediterranean world long preceding Nan Madol's history.

Nan Madol was a sacred city, practicing a cloudy religion.

Whether it was practiced continuously and with very little change from generation to generation cannot be determined. Its practice, though, was not far-flung. The society of the island offered few innovations of distinction; its arts were confined to those found elsewhere in Micronesia. An art that has descended to the present is wood carving. Nan Madol, and Ponape, never mastered stone carving and decoration found elsewhere in the Pacific, especially among the Polynesians. This is the more curious, because the Ponapeans supposedly handled and worked the huge masses of stone needed for the city. On the other hand, the Polynesians never designed a stone city, but developed well-carved stone idols found in different eastern islands.

Lastly, of the criteria supplied by Dr. Montagu, Nan Madol was not perpetuated by its builders. Never again did they build or rebuild. The final exception, possibly, being the smaller ruins on Kusaie.

W. W. Taylor, another anthropologist, quoted by Glyn Daniel, states that "Civilization, being a process of long and complex growth, can be thoroughly understood only when studied throughout its entire range; the past is continually needed to explain the present, and the whole to explain the past."

This brings us into the middle of a continuing argument between two different schools of thought. Many experts assert that cultures and inventions can spring up spontaneously around the world when the need arises, although the peoples are distantly separated and without contact with each other. This, they say, is evolution. It is ascribed to the like workings of men's minds under like conditions, and has occurred on numerous occasions. In modern times, inventors, unbeknown to one another, have worked on inventions at the same time and announced their findings almost simultaneously.

The other school of thought firmly believes that in the past cultures and inventions spread through word of mouth, blood relationship, and contact through trade, either direct or indirect. These authorities are called diffusionists.

Evolutionists believe that society's features evolved separately and developed independently.

Diffusionists believe that such features spread from one area to another, that they had, in fact, been diffused—by trade, movement of people, or cultural contact.

Probably a culture with outstanding traits is a combination of both schools. Daniel quotes R. H. Lowie: "Evolution . . . lay down amicably beside Diffusion."

Right now we are concerned with the puzzle of Nan Madol. How could primitive people, apparently without precedent, achieve such a monumental engineering work?

chapter
5

Modern man often follows the tendencies of his more primitive ancestors to assign romantic, and sometimes supernatural, answers to a problem that has no immediate explanation. In the nineteenth century, in particular, western Europe hosted a number of romantic cults. Prominent among them was the legend of the lost continent of Atlantis.

On more than one occasion some writers have claimed that Nan Madol was once a great city of the lost continent of Mu, or Lemuria. To understand "Mu," which reportedly stretched across practically all of the Pacific Ocean, one must go back to the beginnings of the Atlantis legend, of which Mu was an aftergrowth.

The lost continent of Atlantis started with the Greek writer and philosopher, Plato (427–347 B.C.). Plato quotes Solon, another Athenian, as his authority. Solon was famous as a statesman; he died in 559 B.C., some 130 years before Plato was born. Plato quoted Solon, but unfortunately there is no evidence that Solon's questionable story ever existed. Furthermore, no traces of the story of Atlantis are found in prehistoric Greek tradition, nor have they ever been discovered in the records of Egypt, Phoenicia, Babylonia or Sumeria.

This proves not that no account ever existed, but merely that no account has survived. This is a bit startling when we realize the importance of such a civilization as Atlantis and the activities of the scribes in those ancient Mediterranean societies. If Atlantis had existed, how could all the other writers and historians have ignored reports of it?

Without going into lengthy detail, Atlantis was supposed to be the home of an advanced civilization some 78,000 years ago. Vaguely described, it was "a land lying beyond the Strait of Gibraltar." Such a location equally describes the Azores Islands, the Canary Group, and portions of Africa. It might also include South America, which some traders of the Classical era may have touched.

Atlantis' capital was a great and magnificent stone-walled city circled with moats and canals. Its people were happy and contented, and advanced beyond belief. After Atlantis was devastated by a great disaster, the refugee Atlantans scattered and became the ancestors of the modern Aryans.

For several centuries following Plato's story, other Greek writers were cautious about accepting it, although they did not come right out and deny it. It was not until later that the Romans began to take the story seriously. Still later, other writers picked up the story and scattered the mythical islands around the Atlantic Ocean.

The old Greeks were familiar with the idea of lands emerging from or sinking into the sea. Herodotus (fifth-century B.C. Greek historian) observed fossil seashells in land formations and correctly deduced that the land had once been covered by water. The Greeks generally believed that Sicily had been torn loose from Italy by an earthquake and the Strait of Gibraltar opened by another.

They also held a number of deluge legends which might be traced back to the very ancient Sumerian legend based on real floods in the Euphrates Valley.

Modern scholars believe that Plato's dialogues never were intended, and never pretended to be, an accurate transcript of a real discussion. Often he used pseudomyths to prove a point; he also quoted other supposed experts, putting words in their mouths. Both Socrates (470?–399 B.C.) and Gorgias, a Greek sophist, objected to this technique of Plato's. The fact that Plato assured his readers that his Atlantis story was not a fable, but "genuine history" is simply a literary device still used by modern writers. The same is true of the "old manuscript"—supposedly discovered and quoted—something straight out of Edgar Allan Poe.

Plato was a good storyteller, well educated, who used his imagination to embellish his material. He did not consider himself to be lying; he was composing fictional allegories, and so were his comtemporaries.

The basis for the Atlantis story, according to Plato, was Solon, who supposedly visited Egypt. While there, Egyptian priests first enlightened the visiting Greek concerning the lost civilization. The Egyptians boasted that they had kept records far longer than any other country. This was true; Egypt did have a history, partly inaccurate and with many gaps, going back three thousand years before Plato. But this still left a yawning hole in time of six thousand years if the Egyptians tried to go all the way back to Atlantis. Unfortunately, no one will ever know whether the priests did give Solon such information; some authorities doubt that Solon, in his travels, ever visited Egypt.

Anyhow, proponents of Atlantis maintain that the continent sank beneath the ocean in a huge, catastrophic, geological upheaval about fifteen thousand years ago, leaving only a few small islands to testify to its former existence. This devastation was due to volcanic action. Another group of theorists believe that, equidistant in the past, the icecaps melted at the poles raising the levels of the oceans. The catastrophes that followed are recorded in the flood legends common throughout the Mediterranean area.

Plato could not have been describing a real event, in any literal sense, because according to all geographical evidence his Atlantis "continent" never existed—and no continent ever disappeared (or could!) in the way he described. Arguments of Atlantis theorists to prove the Atlantic origin of civilization from cultural similarities between various peoples are quite useless. These arguments are based on mistaken ideas of archaeology, anthropology, mythology, linguistics and associated sciences. They contain no merit; they cannot be swallowed whole.

Although Plato knew very little about geology and anthropology, the fiction he wrote has continued to haunt Western literature and thought. Much of the pro-Atlantis support, founded on geology, precedes 1900 and is now completely out of date. Geologists have changed their thinking greatly in the last seventy-five years.

While there may have been lost continents, they had nothing to do with Plato's tale, because of the time factor. Geological changes take place over millions of years and do not happen as Plato described. In addition, the oral traditions of primitive man could not preserve the memory of such changes long enough to matter.

"Lost" continents and "forgotten" civilizations are not the same. A continent is a vast area of land; a civilization may occupy a much smaller, limited area and can disappear for other than catastrophic reasons—for instance, Crete and Tartessus; we have already mentioned the Hittites.

There have been instances of tremendous earthquake damage in the Mediterranean such as the eruption of the island of Thera (Santorin) about 1400 B.C. Also named Santorini, it is said to have been part of Atlantis. In this instance, the island is a mere speck of land and not a continental land area.

Regardless, the legend of Atlantis continued from classical times through the medieval ages. Interest was revived with the discovery of America. Spanish historians suggested that Atlantis and America were one and the same. Even as late as 1689, French cartographers published maps of America showing how the new continent compared with Atlantis. This theory had a following among English writers too, including Sir Francis Bacon. The legend kept going through the middle of the nineteenth century.

Dr. Frank C. Hibben, noted anthropologist, says: "The legend of Atlantis is supported by no geological or archeological facts either in Europe or America."

A very recent expedition (1976) conducted by famed underwater explorer, Jacques Cousteau, around Santorini found no support for the Atlantis theory, either. For thirteen months Cousteau made descents in a mini-submarine looking for traces of Atlantis, of which, supposedly, at one time the island had been a part. The explorer told a news conference: "There is nothing whatsoever there to be found. Everything is covered with lava and nothing can ever be found." The expedition, however, did find numerous ancient artifacts, some three thousand years old. Cousteau said he was convinced the story about Atlantis was begun by Plato. He explains: "Plato was the theoretician behind the creation of an ideal state, and he built up a fantasy of Atlantis as his model for a perfect civilization. Atlantis was never a reality, but the myth was carried on after Plato." The destruction which was said to have been a tremendous volcanic eruption and a titanic 500-foot tidal wave would have been "history's greatest explosion."

Why have we given so much attention to the story of Atlantis? Because, in its own place, Atlantis is important to the rise of another "lost" continent—Mu. And Mu has sometimes been advanced as a solution to the mystery of Nan Madol.

The origins of Mu are more murky than those of Atlantis. Possibly followers of the Atlantis theory decided that, if Atlantis was a good idea, then the theory of Lemuria would be even better.

As a result of Darwinian theories advanced by the English naturalist in the nineteenth century, some British geologists noted similarities of formations in India and South Africa. William T. Blanford postulated a possible land bridge called "Gondwana." A German biologist, Ernst H. Haeckel (1887), suggested that this sunken land might be the original home of man because of fossil forms possibly intermediary between men and apes.

Then another Britisher, Philip Sclater, a zoologist, suggested the name of "Lemuria" for this land bridge.

"Lemuria" disappeared—if it ever existed—in the Cenozoic Age. This age ended between one million and ten million years ago, so it had little to do with either Atlantis or the peoples of the Pacific, but it is still being exploited by cultists and occultists for their own purposes.

Oddly enough, the National Geographic Society recently announced that Dr. Robert M. West and Dr. Mary R. Dawson found fossil evidence indicating that a land bridge once spanned the northern Atlantic Ocean between North America and Europe. The lost continental connection stretched between the northernmost tips of Greenland and Spitsbergen, an island north of Scandinavia, and probably split apart between 45 and 48 million years ago. Unfortunately, this is so far back in time that it is useless for even the most rabid cultists.

Returning to Lemuria, we find that later followers moved Lemuria from the Indian Ocean, where it had been located by Blanford, Haeckel, Sclater, *et al.*, several thousand miles into the central Pacific. Now fantasies worked overtime. Lemuria was a vast land mass consisting of three major portions narrowly separated by straits of water. The three areas made up a continent extending from north of Hawaii south to Easter Island and west to the Fiji islands to form a continent 5,000 miles east to west, and 3,000 miles north to south. In this vast land, "civilization" first dawned about 78,000 years ago. It supported a population of 64 million inhabitants living in seven large cities. Very highly civilized, it was the center of all of earth's great civilizations, including India, Babylonia, Persia, Egypt, and Yucatan, which eventually sprang from it. However, this homeland was destroyed by fire, earthquakes, ash falls and trembling volcanoes. Almost all of it sank amid quakes of world-shaking violence.

Naturally, the natives who could migrated. They developed new civilizations that are now beneath the Atlantic, as well as ones in the Mediterranean, India, and a few mountaintops projecting from the Pacific. The major cataclysm forcing the migrations occurred about 26,000 years ago.

To quote Dr. Hibben again: "It is unfortunate that such a tasty bit of evidence as a continent of such proportions should sink beneath the ocean waters and so escape scientific investigation." Dr. Hibben points out, too, that the South Sea Islands have already been shown to be among the last places in the whole Pacific area to have been populated by humans, and yet these same islands are supposedly the remnant mountaintops of Mu.

How did "Mu" come about? In 1864, an erratic French scholar, the Abbé Charles-Étienne Brasseur, traveled widely in South America. In trying to decipher a Mayan alphabet he came upon two symbols which he could not identify and in desperation the good abbé concluded they stood for "M" and "U." *Voilà!* The submerged land of "Mu."

Occultists base their thinking on "inspiration," "tradition," and "insight." They cite folk-memory, myths and legends, and state that every myth has a background of reality.

In the 1870's Helena P. Blavatsky, an occultist of doubtful background, jumped into the Lemuria story. In a wild and weird version, she concocted a theory combining Lemuria with Atlantis. Madame Blavatsky's tasty morsel contained a mixture of the occult, spiritualism, philosophy and mythology. Although she quickly gained a large group of followers, Madame became discredited when solid scholars went to work on her theories. Others, however, picked up her work and carried on.

Many cultists believe in occult meaning of symbols. Thus, a symbol found in one society if identified with a symbol in another society means a relationship. Far-fetched or not! James Churchward, an American writer, wrote a book about the lost continent of Mu in 1926. He believed that a rectangle stood for the letter *M* in the Muvian alphabet and also for *Mu* itself. Subsequently, *any* rectangle (even a tile or a brick) was derived from Mu.

Like other proponents of the Mu theory before him, Churchward's conception was that of a great Pacific continent that stretched from Hawaii to the Fijis, and from Easter Island to the Marianas. A large fertile country, Mu supported a population of 64 million people, divided into ten tribes, covering all colors of the human race, with the whites predominant. (The methods used to arrive at these figures are as mysterious as the continent itself.) Mu sent out colonies and some of the emigrants reached Atlantis via South America and others settled in Asia.

Then, about 13,000 years ago, the "gas belts" in great caves beneath the earth's surface supporting the continents collapsed and let both Mu and Atlantis sink into the oceans and made mountains on the other continents. The Muvians who survived this extraordinary disaster crowded on the small islands of Polynesia—and returned to the level of savages.

The Muvian civilization supposedly existed for about 52,000 years before its destruction and shared with Atlantis the credit for the discoveries of iron, bronze and other metal working, pottery, sculpture, marine navigation, writing, weaving and almost all the other human niceties and achievements you can name.

Occasionally, the idea of a sunken continent receives a little support from nature, to the benefit of the occultists, although the support is greatly exaggerated. A cataclysm may be defined as a violent physical change in the earth's surface, including sudden upheaval, inundation and volcanic activity. Inundation is usually associated with *tsunami*—Japanese for "tidal wave." These waves are sometimes capable of traveling at very high speeds. Such a wave recently damaged Anchorage, Alaska, as well as coastal California towns. For a continent as large as Mu—which supposedly included areas of Australia, New Zealand, the Philippines and other vast parts of Oceania—a tidal wave, regardless of its size, even an impossible 500 feet high, simply could not inundate it.

An idea of the earth's geology is important in evaluating claims of cataclysmic destruction. The earth is, first, a crust of rock. The deeper the crust extends, the hotter it becomes, until 50–100 miles below the surface it is white-hot, molten, and under tremendous pressure. The pressure keeps it as stiff as glass, which resists quick stresses like a solid, but yields like a liquid when required. From 100 miles down, this material becomes "magma"—stiffer than steel and continues to a nickel-iron core about 3,500–4,000 miles in diameter.

The outer crust, first described, is made up of dense rocks such as basalt—mostly silicon and magnesium salts—and lighter rocks like granite—mostly silicon and aluminum, and various others. The heavy rocks are called *sima* ("silicon-magnesium"), and the lighter ones are *sial* ("silicon-aluminum").

Land areas are mostly sial; sea bottoms are sima. Sial rocks on an island may indicate that it was formerly part of a larger island area. On the other hand, islands made up of volcanic sima may signify that they are the result of volcanoes. All the true islands of Polynesia (not including atolls) are volcanic-sima types. This is true of Micronesia with Ponape, Kusaie, and a few others.

Modern geologists believe that a large sinking continent would displace enough water to submerge the other continents—which certainly was not what happened in Oceania.

It is possible for volcanic eruptions to make drastic changes over a number of square miles very quickly, but changes on a continental scale take millions of years.

Either earthquakes or volcanoes can change the topography of the land or submerge it beneath the sea. An event receiving worldwide publicity occurred in 1883, when the island of Krakatoa was destroyed by a gigantic volcanic eruption. The island, 1,400 feet high, sank and was covered by water 1,900 feet deep. However, the island was only 14 square miles in size!

The world has two large earthquake belts. The first, which includes Micronesia, is a horseshoe-shaped zone extending from New Zealand to New Guinea, up to Japan, then across to Alaska, and down California to Chile. The other belt branches off in the East Indies and extends westward to the Himalayas, Iran and southern Europe.

Islands have risen and sunk during geological times, and shallow seas have invaded and retreated from continents. But, geologists do not believe that any great continents ever existed, or will exist, in the central Pacific. And no entire continent has ever disappeared.

A large island, very flat, rising only a few feet above sea level, *might* be submerged by an extremely powerful earthquake, but probably at no more than a few hundred square miles at a clip. Actually, it would not completely disappear, but would remain as a shoal or a bank.

A Geophysical Report, for 1973, gives a worldwide account of twelve earthquakes of a 7.0 magnitude or more, sixteen volcanic eruptions, two cases of bad flooding, and one land slip. In 1972, thirteen earthquakes and twelve volcanic actions were reported. Each year the geophysical activities remain fairly constant.

Dr. Buck stated: "Geologists have found no evidence to support the theory of extensive lands that have sunk within the Polynesian triangle during the periods of man's existence."

However, as we shall see next, science and facts do not stop the fantasy makers who are still active today.

chapter

6

Fantasy makers! As a detective searching through books, reports and other material trying to find clues to the mystery of Nan Madol, I stumble on some astonishing information and misinformation. The myth of Mu dies hard.

As recently as 1975, a book, more or less occult in nature and described by its publishers as "an indestructible time capsule of antiquity," a "mysterious challenge to modern science," and a "prophetic warning of the future," concerns itself, slightly, with Nan Madol. To quote from this book:

> ... the islands of Oceania are dotted with the ruins of some ancient and generally unexplained culture. These stone ruins of the Lemurian civilization were obviously not built by the island peoples living there today. [Author's Note: Agreed, the Ponapeans did not build them, but neither did the Lemurians!] On Ponape, one of the Caroline Islands, there are ruins of a city that could conceivably have housed more than a million inhabitants. Today there are less than 50,000 inhabitants on all the Carolines.

One million inhabitants? Confined within 175 acres? Unless my figures are wrong, that equals 5,715 cramped, crowded, and unidentified citizens per acre! The only way to accommodate such a large number would be the erection of towering skyscrapers. The best evidence shows that the old Nan Madol engineers built as high as 30 feet, and even possibly, a little higher. But a skyscraper? We will continue with the fairy tale:

> It is pointed out in *The Ultimate Frontier* that this ancient city is called Metalanim [*sic*], and the ruins indicate it was built of gigantic stone blocks weighing up to fifteen tons apiece. The stone used is not found on the islands today. [Author's Note: The basalt-crystal "logs" are found in a number of quarries on the island today.] Referring to Metalanim, *The Ultimate Frontier* says: "Artificial waterways capable of passing a modern battleship [*sic!*] intersect the city. Metalanim is remarkable for its architectural and engineering excellence and is not at all like the primitive works one associates with the natives of Oceania ... This city was apparently built by the people of Lemuria of rock hewn from now submerged lands."

Well, first of all, Nan Madol is *not* Matolenim. Matolenim is *not* a city, it is an ancient divisional territory of the island of Ponape, to which Nan Madol is attached. The old rulers of Matolenim resided in Nan Madol.

Regarding the canals permitting passage of battleships, if the battleship were not longer than a canoe, were not more than six feet wide, and drew no more than a few inches of water, it *might* get through. The canals are narrow and winding, and although today they are almost entirely silted up, when cleaned out they never exceeded more than a few feet in depth.

So far as architectural and engineering excellence is concerned, it is difficult for the eye of a beholder to find it. What is impressive is the sheer magnitude of the tremendous effort in quarrying, moving the materials, and erecting the city. The

The famed canals of Nan Madol are narrow, crooked and muddy.
Many of them are filled with silt, but some can accommodate a
flat-bottomed boat or a light canoe. Most explorers of the city
find it faster and more convenient to wade through the shallow,
muddy channels. It is said that at one time the bottom of the
canals were paved with stone blocks. As the photo shows, jungle
underbrush and shrubs have taken over the banks.

This typical section of stone wall is between twenty and thirty feet
high. It is possible that, when erected, some of the walls may have
measured fifty or more feet. Today, the remaining stretches are
littered at their bases with loose stones from the crumbling walls.

builders used no arches, keystones, or buttresses and made little (if any) effort at decoration. The great stone logs were not worked or joined; they were fitted together most crudely. What a visitor to the ruins receives is an impression of great primitive strength, not beauty of design.

If, as Lemuria's proponents urge, Lemuria was a great seat of culture and achievement, it would appear logical that Lemurian builders would have refined their crafts beyond the primitive level exhibited in Nan Madol.

Continuing from the same source:

... Metalanim is not merely an isolated archeological mystery, there are remnants of forty stone temples of similar architectural design located on barren Malden Island some 3,000 miles from Ponape. Roadways of basalt blocks lead off in every direction from the temples and vanish into the Pacific. Ruins of the same type of roadway can be found on almost all of the islands of Oceania within the ring of fire.

As I have detailed before, similar ruins, although smaller and even cruder, do exist on the island of Kusaie, about 300 miles east and south of Nan Madol. The Malden Island, to which he refers, is indeed 3,000 miles east of Ponape and is one of the Line group of islands. To compare the huge buildings of Nan Madol as "of similar architectural design" to the small platforms used on Malden Island for religious purposes is utterly ridiculous. The platforms on Malden are small enclosures approximately 6 feet by 6 feet by 3 feet high. Any structure on Malden could have been built by fifty men. The "paved roads" disappearing in the sea are simply paths for fishermen, laid with stepping stones, or flagstones, for wet weather.

It should be apparent that neither of the occult writers quoted ever saw or visited Nan Madol, but—like cooks in a poor diner—picked up a recipe from some source and just kept adding to it.

Dr. Paul Hambruch, who led the first German expedition to study Nan Madol in 1908–1910, published a report maintaining that construction of the city was of comparatively recent times and Nan Madol was not deserted, or evacuated, until about two hundred years before he saw it. Dr. Hambruch also stated that the city was a ceremonial center to practice a religion centered around the worship of a turtle god.

If this date for the decease of the city is true, then it remained in existence until around 1700 A.D. But, certainly, it must have been built long before that time; an enterprise of such gigantic size would require several generations, or more, to accomplish, depending on the manpower available. The 1963 Smithsonian expedition set a date of 1285 A.D., based on carbon dating, but again, this does not prove that the city was built at that time. Nan Madol might have been very, very old in 1285; the carbon-dated material merely proves that the practice of a religion based on sacred turtles was being practiced by that time. Dr. Hambruch's report long preceded the use of carbon-14 dating.

However, both Dr. Hambruch's observation of a turtle cult, and the Smithsonian's establishing an early existence of such a cult are extremely interesting.

A turtle cult is a valuable clue to follow and examine more closely.

The sacred turtle is not unique to the Ponapeans. However, it is not exactly commonplace, either. The turtle, or tortoise, is usually a mythical animal on which the world rests, and such belief is found in Asia, Europe and America.

In India, the *Satapathe Brahmana,* as early as 600 B.C., uses the turtle as an important emblem of creative power. Kurma is the foundation, at the bottom of the Sea of Milk, on which the creative pillar is reared in the age of reality. Vishnu sits on the top of Mandara, or shaft of the world, which rests on the back of Kurma—"the maker." Vishnu is the creator, and Kurma is called "the turtle-shaped one."

In the Hindu religion, Kurma is also called Kaura, or Kachcha-pa, and Kasyape, "the first born of time." As Kachcha-pa, the turtle is considered the first of the nine treasures of Kuvera—the god of wealth.

The religion of the Hindus is a complicated one, and interpretations are difficult without long and involved explanations—something I am trying to avoid. But we should be satisfied concerning Nan Madol. So, in another incarnation, Vishnu appears as a tortoise to stir up the Sea of Milk from which the world of animated beings was to be created. The Hindu epithet of "Kacyopas" applied to the tortoise means "the lord, the guardian of the shores, he who occupies the shores."

On a less exalted level in the Far East, the turtle had a significance in a cosmic implication: its shell was rounded on top, to represent heaven, and was flat underneath to represent the earth. Everyone, of high or low degree, could see this. And the turtle became an emblem of longevity.

The old Greeks, too, had a myth in which the turtle obtained from Zeus himself the power to conceal itself under its own shield and carry its house along with it.

Perhaps the details of the turtle worship conducted in Nan Madol may never become known. But an explanation, as offered by a modern Ponapean, is interesting. I asked him why a turtle might be considered sacred; why the old inhabitants of the island would worship it in the belief that it had magical powers. In not too fluent English he explained: When a turtle is caught and killed, its lower shell is split open. Although dead, the muscles across the turtle's chest continue to stretch and contract, flex, for a period of time afterward. The old Ponapeans believed that this proved the turtle was still alive although it was also evident that it had been killed—that it was dead. In a very primitive form this was an example of life after death.

One of the ten stars of the constellation of the Tortoise, situated in the northern heavens, in the autumnal sky, and especially ruled by the moon, was called the *Lyre* by the Greeks. The fable held that the tortoise, from whose shell Hermes had made the lyre, had been transfigured into the constellation.

An interesting historical side note regards the ancient Kassites, whom the old Greek writers knew well. The Kassites lived in a mountainous region east of Babylon, and in 1780 B.C. they founded a Babylonian dynasty that lasted 570 years.

In the eleventh century B.C., a turtle appears to take the place of the Zodiacal Crab (the fourth month) on a Kassite boundary stone.

Some centuries later, when Zoroastrianism appeared in Persia (sixth to seventh century B.C.) the tortoise was considered an evil creature and, consequently, to be killed. A turtle was also considered taboo in Madagascar and Java until modern times.

Turtle worship was not nearly so extensive as serpent worship. However, groups of Polynesians had legends pertaining to turtle-people in their oral histories. Too, when Polynesians caught turtles at sea, a piece of the breast bone was immediately detached and offered with an incantation to Tangaroa— god of the sea and fishermen. Only the principal chief and priest ate the turtle's heart and flipper. Turtle meat was taboo to women.

Halfway around, on the opposite side of the world, we again find the turtle. This time on money. The Greek island of Aegina furnished the ancient world with great sailors, who sailed the length and breadth of the Mediterranean—and probably beyond. Aegina was a "free port" and was known by traders everywhere.

Aegina's coins bore an effigy of the turtle. Although the island was small—only about 41 square miles, with a population of fewer than five thousand citizens—the turtle coins were accepted without question everywhere in the Classical world. A possible explanation for the choice of device on the coin is that the Aeginetans practiced a restrained form of advertising; giant sea turtles are an easily identifiable form of marine life, and whoever saw an Aeginetan coin instantly recognized it as a symbol of the seafarers who ranged far and wide, as did the turtle.

Another explanation offers a Greek adaptation from the Egyptian. In Egyptian paintings, the turtle is the symbol for marine life. The Aeginetan sailors may have liked the idea and used it; perhaps they believed that it brought them luck.

The use of a turtle in religion, or for other reason, is not unique to any one area of the world. It has been said that

American Mound Builders, in prehistoric times, erected a turtle-effigy mound.

As stated earlier, not too many details are known concerning the practice of the turtle religion in Nan Madol. Eels were kept on the isle of Idehd and once a year a high ceremony was performed in which four turtles at a time were baked and fed to them. From the way the eels snatched at the proffered food, a priest was supposed to make divinations.

Both fresh- and saltwater eels are found in Ponape. They are large and vicious. Extremely savage, they are still greatly respected by present-day Ponapeans. Some eels live in the freshwater lakes of the mountains; they too are deadly. The older generations of islanders never referred to the eel by name—this was taboo. It was usually addressed as Kamichik, which means "Terrible One."

Why the combination of eel and turtle for religious purposes? Guesses can be made. For fishermen to capture a live eel presents a dangerous achievement. It is both difficult and hazardous. In a way, it might be the equivalent of a Medal of Honor. Because of its large, thick, repulsive appearance, an eel could easily become a superstitious symbol of evil—a true-life representative of angry and vengeful gods. Other than a shark, no more dangerous denizen of the South Seas can be found than an eel.

On the other hand, the sea turtles are both impressive and peaceful. Some grow as large as five hundred pounds or more. They sleep afloat one to two feet below the surface of the water and can be captured by spearing them through the shoulder. Their meat is considered a delicacy. Possibly an offering from such a peaceful giant is just the right gift to a vengeful and malign spirit. It should also be remembered that for ages past, in Oceania, tortoise shell was very valuable for making household utensils, such as scrapers of coconut meat, as well as combs, jewelry and ornaments.

chapter

7

Nan Madol does not offer us many facts from which to make strong logical deductions. Dr. Hambruch believed that the city dated back only to around the start of the seventeenth century; the Smithsonian Institution carbon-dated remains at around 1285 A.D. Other authorities have pushed back its founding to 700–900A.D. This allows for a difference spanning approximately one thousand years. To add to the debate, other experts believe the city was founded more than two thousand years ago, thus antedating the Christian era.

Unfortunately, carbon-14 dating does not work on stone. Stone is already old, millions of years old, so it is useless to find its age, and there is no technique for ascertaining the date of its use in the construction in question. Carbon-14 dating is extremely valuable when used on organic substances— bones (human or animal), pottery, shells, middens, skins, leather, writing materials, charcoal and refuse. As I know, very few organic remains have ever been found in Nan Madol.

History, however, tells me something to remember:

> Where documentary evidence is lacking, we can make a
> good guess at the original trait from its distribution. If

the trait is found in one continuous area, the chances are that it was diffused from one center. If on the other hand, it occurs in two widely separated places, with no trace of its existence in between, it is likely to have been invented independently in both.

Here is another important note:

Although primitive people may sometimes pick up a culture trait from visitors, when it fits easily into their own pattern, they usually submit to wholesale cultural change only as a result of long contact or overwhelming pressure from a more advanced culture.

I realize that Nan Madol is a unique, planned city of great size and primitive construction. Nothing like it is found anywhere throughout Oceania except on Kusaie. The Polynesians are known to have built walls, platforms, and terraces from stone, but never on a scale even remotely resembling Nan Madol; neither did the Polynesians ever plan and lay out a constructed stone city.

Civilization does not spring up in a day, a month, or a year. It rises from a cruder preceding culture.

Cities are abandoned for a number of reasons—epidemics, earthquakes, volcanoes, floods, climatic changes, war, social decadence and disorder. Perhaps it is important that the Ponapeans, more than most Micronesians, tend toward violence and have a long history of conflicts among clans. Their violence continued, in the face of tremendous odds, in uprisings against former Spanish and German rulers of the island.

Possibly a few islanders may have squatted on an islet or two of the city, and fished in surrounding waters, when the great smallpox epidemic hit the island in 1854. But the city seems to have been long deserted and forgotten by that time. If an earlier epidemic did clear out the population of the capital, it occurred beyond the reach of the Ponapean memory.

Were earthquakes responsible for the city's destruction? When a severe earthquake hits, material such as columns, pillars, facing stone, et cetera, fall out in a marked pattern as is found in Olympia, Greece. In Nan Madol, the walls have been scattered in all directions; from the massive roots of trees and vines growing over the ruins, no traces of an earthquake pattern are apparent. Geologists tell me that some slight earthquakes may have shaken surrounding islands, but nothing to produce great devastation or cause islands to sink.

Today, Ponape with its small surrounding islands—like the other, larger islands in the East Caroline group—does not support a population exceeding 50,000 persons within a radius of 500 miles. Possibly the figure may be considerably less. Increased food supplies and lack of warfare have contributed to the population growth; it is doubtful that in the distant past the population ever came close to this present-day figure. The point is that large reserves of manpower were never readily available in and around Ponape. This is a factor that must always be considered when trying to solve the mystery of the construction of Nan Madol. To offset the lack of a large labor force, as we shall see later, a time factor must be taken into consideration. One advantage the Ponapeans had—and they had plenty of it—was sufficient time.

Researching through the available material on Oceania, searching for historical clues, we find references to India and China as possible sources of the great mixture of peoples in Micronesia and Polynesia.

Ponape lies approximately 2,600 miles east and south of the mainland coast of China. Almost from time immemorial, the Chinese have traded up and down the coast of China and Southeast Asia. The ancient lumbering Chinese junks were magnificently seaworthy and were quite capable of carrying large cargoes on extended voyages. Some anthropologists believe that over a period of several millennia unknown numbers of junks were blown off course during tropical storms, later to drift battered and helpless into the western Pacific. Eventually the junks, with their crews, were shipwrecked or made shore on the scattered Micronesian islands. The intermarriages of these lost crews with the islanders account for the Oriental strain present in many Micronesians—or so it is claimed.

Others maintain that from time to time migrations of varying numbers took place between China and the Micronesian islands. This theory provides the claim that the ancient Chinese *knew* of the existence of land—islands—in that far-off area to which they could migrate. It is entirely possible that the Chinese did know this almost from the dawn of history.

The Chinese possessed an advanced civilization, comparable to the best of the West's, from the most ancient times. Quite by accident, while I was haunting the stacks in libraries, I stumbled upon a most remarkable book. I cannot read Chinese, so what I read was an English translation of *Shan Kai King* (*Classic of Mountains and Seas*). This ancient record was started sometime around 2250 B.C. by a scholar named Yu, who was also the Minister of Public Works serving under the Emperor Shun. Yu served in this public capacity for seventeen years and on Shun's death became emperor.

During Shun's reign, the emperor wanted a geography of the entire world. From his treasury, the emperor outfitted ships with bands of explorers and sailed them off to search, investigate, map and report on new and distant lands. The reports were concluded about 2205 B.C. and consisted of thirty-two books, of which only eighteen are known today. The noun *book* may be misleading; *report* may be more accurate and descriptive. Each report is an entity, but has no beginning or end.

Some of the reports minutely detail geographical features of unnamed lands. Other reports are lyrical and poetical, describing the beauties of nature.

However, one of the reports carries what is believed to be a remarkably accurate description of 2,200 miles of the west coast of North America, including mountain ranges, rivers, lakes, flora, fauna, and almost exactly measured distances from point to point extending from Canada to Central Mexico.

The difficulty in making positive identification of locales and natural geographic features in the report is that the Orientals named them in their own Chinese tongue. Western sailors did the same, thousands of years later, when exploring the Americas, using their own languages (or that of the ruler supporting the expedition)—which accounts for the Spanish, Portuguese, Italian, French, Dutch and English names sprinkled through our atlases. One can sympathize with a research scholar attempting to identify Mount Rainier, in the state of Washington (Indian name: *Tacoma*), with a mountain bearing a Chinese name which translates into something like "gleaming upthrust of stone proudly wearing wreaths of heaven [clouds] on its noble brow." The location and description of lakes, rivers, and other natural formations in the vicinity of the mountain, together with very accurate distances between topographical points of the area may almost convince the specialist that the mountain is the same, but he can't be absolutely *certain!*

Until around 300 B.C., the *Classic of Mountains and Seas* was required reading for serious Chinese students, but then the reports began to be doubted. Such a long period of time had passed since it was compiled, that misinterpretations arose. The Chinese began looking within the boundaries of China for natural wonders of the description contained in the reports, forgetting that the *Shan Kai King* was about other countries.

When the scholars of the third century B.C. failed to find clues in China to identify the described wonders, they decided that the accounts were fictitious, simply good literature. Up to this time, the "books" had been copied and recopied to infinity.

In 213 B.C., during the Ts'in dynasty, all the "books" in China were ordered burned. Some of the books of *Shan Kai King* managed to escape destruction. Later, a few of the lost manuscripts were rewritten from memory; others were condensed.

In the fifth century A.D., another condensation of literary material was ordered by the imperial court. Today we have only the fragments that survived the burning and condensations.

Preceding this final condensation, in the third century B.C., as noted above, when the Chinese scholars could not identify the landmarks and other descriptions in the "books" as being located in their own country, they no longer took the reports seriously. The important point is, however, that up until the third century B.C., for a period of almost two thousand years, the Chinese knew, or believed, that there were other lands beyond the Pacific Ocean to the east.

To quote Hibben again: "As early as 500 B.C., China was trafficking in fossil ivory tusks of Mammoths from Siberia." He continues to point out that much of the early Chinese ivory carving that we consider so typically Chinese was done with this fossil material.

It is obvious, from this ivory trade, that Chinese merchants and traders knew of distant locations as far away as Siberia. It would follow that the Siberians knew of the Bering Strait and the presence of a great land mass (North America) lying just beyond the Strait. Consequently, if there were Chinese migrations, the travelers knew they were not jumping off their own land into an endless expanse of ocean. Even though the migrants might not have known exact distances and locations, they must have realized that, if they journeyed long and far enough, eventually they would find land—whether islands, large or small, or even vast new continents. It should also be remembered that primitive population movements seldom involve mass movements.

The Shang emperors, 1500 B.C., made up the first dynasty of which historians have reliable information. The Chou dynasty ruled from 1122 B.C. to 220 B.C. The Ts'in, mentioned before as ordering all the books in China burned, was also responsible for starting construction of the Great Wall in 220 B.C. This was, and possibly still is, the greatest building feat of all time. The wall was constructed to cross the northern boundary of China from the sea to the far northwest. It was intended to cope with the raids of Mongolian nomads.

Simply to get an idea of its size: in a straight line the wall extends 1,400 miles, but with turns, twists and loops, its length is 2,550 miles. In most places the wall was 30 feet high and 25 feet thick, tapering to 15 feet in width at the top. The top of the wall contained a paved roadway within a 6-foot crenellated parapet.

About each 250 yards, a watchtower straddled the roadway. Each tower was 35 feet square and 45 feet high. In all, there were 25,000 towers and 15,000 additional detached towers. Outside the wall were three ditches filled with water.

Do not let anyone tell you that ancient man did not know how to build. He did, but he also had certain advantages that modern engineers do not have. The Chinese emperor was able to conscript literally hundreds of thousands of workers—artisans, soldiers, criminals and paupers. Farms were laid out along the course of the wall to grow crops so the army of builders had a secure food supply. Time was not of primary importance.

Hypothetically, it is not improbable that the development and expanding state of the Shang dynasty from North China into South China caused widespread social disorder. As the more culturally advanced Shang groups pressed forward, the less advanced coastal groups were forced to vacate their home territories. Over a number of years various small social units moved offshore or further down the coast into Southeast Asia. Eventually their descendants may have reached Indonesia.

Perhaps, at this time, we should take a look at ancient Chinese navigation. The old junks were extremely seaworthy. The Chinese, too, have been credited with the invention of the compass. As early as 1300 B.C., references are found concerning "south-pointing chariots." Modern theory, though, discounts these as compasses. Probably they were a gear mechanism of some kind. The old Chinese knew about gears. However, the first definite allusion to a magnetic needle, in China, appears much later—in 800 A.D. Not until around 1100 A.D. is reference made to a Chinese mariner's compass. Other experts maintain that the Chinese compass was devised in the twelfth century A.D. In the beginning it was used only for journeying by land and indicated south instead of north. So, it is doubtful that, if the ancient Chinese sailors did sail into the Pacific, they navigated with the aid of a compass.

Finally, a brief consideration of the Chinese language is important. It is distinctive. Its use should be traced through migrating groups, especially if the language was used over a wide area for long periods of time. The Chinese tongue has comparatively few sounds. These are combined in a limited number of ways so that only 412 different syllables are possible; one syllable per word. The use of different vocal tones distinguish otherwise identical sounds. As everyone knows,

Chinese writing was extremely complex. At one time it contained 49,000 monosyllabic characters. Today many of the characters have been simplified and condensed.

The Ponapeans, so far as is known, never had a written language. If evidence to the contrary should be found, it is almost a certainty that it would have little connection with Chinese. Regarding the Ponapean spoken tongue, there is little evidence of Chinese.

At this point, all that we can safely determine is that a faint Oriental blood strain is found in the Micronesian mixtures on the islands. Evidence of Chinese culture is practically nonexistent.

Although the ancient Chinese certainly had the engineering skill and know-how to have built the city of Nan Madol, there is no proof that they did.

I will have to look elsewhere.

chapter

8

The great protective wall fronting the approach to Nan Madol is reported to have been at one time 2,811 feet long and 16 feet high. This is well over half a mile in length. I did not measure the wall myself, as I lacked both the skill and equipment to attempt it. The front wall faces in an easterly direction. At right angles, a second similar wall stretches from the southeast corner of the front wall back almost to the shore of Tenwen Island. No wall exists on Tenwen to protect the rear of the city. An attack by way of Tenwen through the thick jungle would have been difficult at best, and defense would have been effective. Perhaps the founders of Nan Madol considered building a rear wall to the city, but the project, for one reason or another, was never completed.

Some estimates put the number of basalt columns and logs used in construction between four and five million. I do not know how this number was reached, as it is impossible to count the pieces individually. But if the actual number is only half that estimated, it is still impressive and compares favorably with the building of the pyramids. The Great Pyramid of Khufu (Cheops) contains 2⅓ million blocks of stone, each averaging 2½ tons in weight. Depending on the manpower available, the erection of Nan Madol might have taken as long as three hundred years! And there is evidence that not all construction had been completed when the city was abandoned.

The building of the city demanded considerable engineering knowledge. We have considered China, but dismissed the possibility because of lack of proof.

Another important possibility exists—India.

Again, we know little about ancient India. In 2000 B.C., when Babylon and Egypt were flourishing, an Indus Valley civilization was also flowering. It lasted from about 2500 B.C. to 1500 B.C. Modern names for the Indus Valley culture are *Harappa* and *Mohenjo Daro*—after its two chief cities. No one has any idea what the people called themselves, nor are we sure whether it was one united kingdom or two affiliated states.

The ruins uncovered by archaeologists show that this ancient civilization of the Indus was well advanced. At its greatest extent it covered a larger area than either Mesopotamia or Egypt. The two main areas centered around the cities of Harappa and Mohenjo Daro. It is probable that the old Harappan ports were involved with trade along the Persian Gulf. The port of Lothal, at the head of the Gulf of Cambay, had a huge burnt-brick dock for shipping. Apparently, from early in their history the Indus people maintained trading contacts with neighbors to the west.

Dress and hair style of the Indus population displayed definite similarities with the old Sumerians. Men wore trimmed beards and long hair rolled in a bun. A light robe was worn, leaving the right shoulder bare. The women wore many necklaces, huge headdresses, miniskirts and ornamental belts around the hips.

Evidence indicates that Indus merchants or their agents were resident in Ur and other Mesopotamian cities. Their boats were high-prowed and single-masted. They knew and used wheeled carts pulled by *zebus*—oxlike, humped, short-horned animals.

Indus prosperity was based on agriculture. The farmers

used irrigation with success to grow cereal crops, oil crops of sesame and mustard, melon, dates, and cotton. Animals included sheep, pigs, dogs and cats—which guarded the great granaries.

Metalsmiths worked copper into spears, knives, and flat axes, but these articles were of a poor quality and probably costly. Commoners still used neatly flaked stone blades and implements. The people also used a pottery wheel, wove cotton cloth, and possibly were excellent woodworkers and carvers.

Indus towns and cities were built on a grid plan of straight streets—the first known appearance of this kind of city planning in the history of civilization. At Mohenjo Daro, streets thirty feet wide ran north and south. Other streets crossed them to form city blocks 1200 by 800 feet in size. These large blocks were subdivided by alleys up to ten feet wide on which the houses opened. Although the streets and alleys were not paved, plenty of public wells were available for the inhabitants. A complete underground drainage system served the city.

In the lower town stood a forty-foot-high artificial mound of mud brick surmounted by a citadel similar to those built by the Assyrians; it was strongly fortified. The city too was probably walled and must have measured a mile square. Harappa was similar.

Such towns can be built only by an absolute authority. And the massive walls, bastions and towers, after they are built, need soldiers to man them. Weapons in use were spears, bows and arrows, axes, slings and daggers.

The Indus engineers did not build great imposing temples or palaces. In Mohenjo Daro, the two outstanding buildings are a large granary and the Great Bath. The very large city granaries probably paid out government wage-rations. A city flour mill where grain was pounded in numbers of wooden mortars is supported by the presence of little, two-room dwellings built to uniform design. These resemble the Egyptian quarters built in support of the pyramids, and in Mohenjo Daro they probably housed a specialized labor force.

The Great Bath is an artificial pool about forty feet long

and waterproofed by bitumen. Broad flights of steps lead into the water at either end. In addition to being used for bathing, the pool possibly was used for some kind of religious purification.

No royal tombs have ever been discovered. There is evidence of a pillared assembly hall, but it lacks a throne room or any other indication of royal prestige. It is unlikely that the Indus state was "democratic" or similar to ancient Greek city-states. Undoubtedly it did have a ruler, but *who* is not known.

Private houses of various sizes were two stories high, substantial in construction and built of brick. They were comfortable. Each house had a bathroom and a privy, often a seated privy. Earthenware pipes carried the waste from both floors into public drains running below the center of the streets. These public drains were neatly and methodically constructed of brick and had inspection holes. There is proof they were periodically cleared of accumulated rubbish and muck.

Some authorities claim that this urban drainage system was unparalleled in pre-Classical times in Europe. It is difficult to think of an example other than the Palace of Knossos in Crete. The "Queen's Bath," as well as the palace, had a drainage system, but not on a citywide scale.

We have gone into quite a detailed account of the Indus builders. Few can doubt that the old Indus engineers knew how to build. One fact stands out, though, in our search for the builders of Nan Madol. Or, rather, it is the *lack* of a fact. The Indus construction was all of well-bonded brick; no stone was used. Certainly not the monolithic stones found on Ponape. Indus architecture tapered walls upward, as did the Egyptians; the corbel was known and used, but no true arches. Only a very few examples of stone sculpture have been found—crude squatting figures possibly in a religious attitude.

It is interesting to discover that among all the great primary civilizations of the world, except possibly that of the Incas, no comparably sized powerful civilization shows such a poverty of artistic achievement. This lack is one reason it is so difficult for the experts to figure out religious, political and social backgrounds of the Indus people.

Some art has been found. One small figurine is quite famous; about seven inches tall, it represents a male figure often designated as a "priest-king." No one knows for sure. Another bronze is a diminutive dancing girl, naked except for arm bangles, and in a brazen, almost defiant, stance. She is both beautiful and marvelously realistic. Art experts sometimes maintain the little female figure shows a superficial look of Greek influence.

The Harappans were very good at carving animals, and modeled little monkeys in terra cotta. They made really fine intaglio carvings of sacred animals for steatite seals. Some of the seals show scenes of bull-baiting and leaping, with a shrine enclosing a sacred tree and incorporating a sacred pillar. This naturally leads to parallels of similar scenes found in ancient Crete.

Elaborate bead necklaces, usually of faience, but some of semiprecious stones such as jade indicate contact with Central Asia or Burma. Too, there are gold disk beads much like those found at Troy and Ur.

None of the refinements of civilization in the Indus have been discovered in Nan Madol. Yet, possibly, a very tenuous connection might have existed—some way, somehow—between the peoples of the Indus and Micronesia and Polynesia. From the mouth of the Indus River, in present-day Pakistan, to Easter Island in the far-eastern Pacific, is approximately 13,000 miles as the crow flies! Easter Island (Rapa Nui) is famous for the gigantic stone-head monuments and *rongo-rongo* writing found there. It is the farthest east of all the Polynesian islands lying closest to the west coast of South America.

Rongo-rongo is unique—found nowhere else in the world, *except* possibly in the old Indus civilization. Experts have been unable to decipher either of the scripts. We will examine both, later, in another chapter. What is remarkable is that both "alphabets," or characters are so similar. And in some instances are *identical*. The number of identical characters is too large to be a coincidence. Carrying the "coincidence" even further is a less distinct, but still evident, similarity of both scripts to the ancient Linear B, discovered in Crete.

The question remains: *Who* were the people of the Indus Valley civilization? Some authorities believe that the *idea* of civilization came to the Indus Valley from Mesopotamia. The Harappans used a standard of weights and measures and, as mentioned above, had a script, although they left very few written records. Whatever writing has been found is limited to short inscriptions with no more than seventeen signs or characters—mostly on seals, pottery, and small copper amulets.

Two schools of thought exist regarding the original inhabitants of the Indus Valley civilization. One school, basing its theory on skeletal evidence dug up by archaeologists, maintains that the Harappans were of two distinct types: (1) the majority of the population had fairly long heads, marked brow ridges, were tall and probably "Caucasi"; (2) the minority was slightly less tall, even more dolichocephalic and best identified as "Mediterranean" racial stock.

The other group of experts assert that from prehistoric times a "pre-Aryan" people called *Dravidians* lived in parts of southern India. Their native name and language was Tamil. These people had watched ships arrive from the West . . . from the far-eastern Mediterrannean . . . and had loaded them for their return journey with cargo the Tamils had brought back from China and Ceylon in their own ships.

The name given to the men of the sea (Greeks) who came out of the West was "Ionians." In the Tamil language this was: "Yona, Yonaka, and Yavana." In their own tongue, the sound *Y* equals *I*. This appellation was used as far back, perhaps, as the sixth century B.C. These dates, of course, are centuries later than the rise and fall of the Indus civilization. Proponents of the Dravidian theory, however, assert these Tamils were descendants of the builders of the Indus Valley state(s). Historical Dravidians are dark-skinned, resulting, possibly, from intermarriage with Negroid peoples when the Dravidians were driven out of their original homelands by invaders.

Around 1750 B.C., the Aryans—war-like, barbaric nomads—overran northwest India. They extended their rule across the north of India, down the Ganges Valley to the Sea of Bengal. It is probable that the Aryans attacked the Harappan people between 1700 and 1650 B.C. Mohenjo Daro may have held on for another 150 years before it too fell. The ancient civilization disappeared from the course of history, although small isolated groups may have held together for generations afterward.

In the areas the Aryans conquered, the cultural level declined. The Harappans had been far more civilized, which may have accounted for their downfall, as they were not a warlike people and their weapons were inferior to the invaders'.

The religion of the Aryans is unknown, as is that of the Harappans. Possibly the Aryans took over the "caste" system already existing among the Indus people. A combination of two religions is not unusual between conquered and conquering peoples—and such a combination evolved into the forerunner of the Brahman (or Hindu) religion in India today.

There is some evidence that the Indus divinity may have been a prototype of Siva, the great god of historic India. The bull is one aspect of Siva as *Pasupati* ("Lord of Beasts"). I have also pointed out a similarity to the old Cretan practice of bull worship. And let me not forget Vishnu and his aspect as a sacred turtle.

After the Aryan conquest, writing did not enter into wide use for many centuries. And what records might have existed did not survive. Paper from palm fronds does not last long in extreme climates amid abundant insect life, and the Indians themselves showed little interest in history. By 300 B.C., though, there was an Aryan alphabet in India based on a Greek reformed alphabet of the Phoenicians from around 700 B.C.

I have pressed to find in the Indus Valley clues that might have some connection with the object of my pursuit, Nan Madol. The Indus civilization produced no monumental or large-scale stone decorative work. It might possibly have had a wood-carving tradition; but, as this is all lost, it cannot be proved. Numerous terra cotta figures of the "mothergoddess" type have been unearthed. Also very crude and grotesque little animal figurines. These may have been used as votive offerings. No such votive offerings have been found at Nan Madol.

What I have found may or may not be important. It is open to misinterpretation and overtheorizing. Nan Madol and the Indus both held the turtle sacred. The Indus and Easter Island used a script of similar appearance; it is possible that this "script" might have reached the end of Polynesia via sea journeys through Micronesia. Both held several animals in common: the pig and the dog. The Indus had the zebu, the sheep, and the cat, which the Micronesians did not have; the Micronesians had chickens. Cotton weaving, pottery and metalworking were unknown on Ponape, as were many of the Indus' agricultural plants and crops.

One clue that I have kept in mind while continuing the search is the ancient Greeks. As history tells us, the Greeks seemed to have had their fingers in most everything. As we have seen, there is evidence that their influence was not unknown in India at a very early date. Of course, 33 centuries passed between the end of the Indus Valley civilization and the discovery of Nan Madol by Westerners.

A great deal can happen in 3,300 years.

chapter

9

One of the common and most pressing questions regarding Nan Madol is: How could an ancient and primitive people, without tools, erect such a heavy mass of material into a city?

I have a pretty good idea how it was accomplished; what I do not know is when and why. The old Egyptians, when they built their pyramids, left an excellent blueprint. Tomb paintings illustrate their techniques in detail.

The Great Pyramid of Khufu (Cheops) was built in 2900 B.C. This huge construction is 756 feet square and rises to a height of 480 feet—equivalent to a forty-story building. It is made up of over 2,300,000 blocks of stone, weighing an average of 2½ tons. The builders used limestone from local outcrops, and outer casings of fine limestone from east of Cairo.

It has been estimated that the tremendous cathedrals of Milan and Florence, St. Paul's Basilica in Rome and Westminster Abbey could all fit within its boundaries. The pyramid probably contains somewhere between five and six million tons of stone!

The Egyptians used the corbeled arch and vault before the true arch and vault were discovered. The corbel is one of four devices used by the old builders. The others were the post and lintel; the arch and vault; and the truss. Brick and stone are the best materials for construction of the corbel, arch and vault. Stone and wood were used for post and lintel, a construction favored by the Greeks. Wood alone was used for the truss.

Herodotus said that it took 100,000 laborers, working three-month shifts, twenty years to build the Great Pyramid. This however, is not true; it is greatly exaggerated.

In addition to tomb paintings, other sources—tool marks, quarries, and even the ancient tools themselves—give us additional information. The only metal tools the Egyptians had were copper; they made little use of the wheel and may not even have used rollers; they probably lacked pulleys.

A painting in a tomb shows 172 men pulling a 60-ton statue on a sled without rollers! An advance man poured milk, oil or fat on the ground in front of the sled to lubricate its passage. In Khufu's time, crews handled 2½-ton blocks and a number of granite slabs weighing over 50 tons each. By the time of Menkaure (2600–2500 B.C.) the Egyptians were building with stones weighing over 50 tons each. In Rameses II's reign (1292–1225 B.C.) the builders moved 1,000-ton statues!

How were the Egyptians able to quarry such enormous stones? Probably in a manner similar to that of the Ponapeans. The Egyptians cut notches in the rock, at the quarry, along the line of a natural fracture. Then they drove wooden wedges into the notches. Next, the wedges were wetted down with water. When the wood swelled, the block split off. Or after the stakes dried, they were lighted by fire. Another method was for the crews to pound at the rock with balls of hard diorite (stone). They bashed out a trench all around the stone to be detached. Experiments have shown that this type of labor could lower the level of a stone at the rate of ⅕ inch per hour.

After the rocks were quarried, crews used levers and ramps to get the stones on sleds, then to move the sleds to the building site. The Egyptians used enormous ropes of palm fiber or reed. If, as a tomb painting indicates, 172 men could move a 60-ton stone, then 8 men should be able to move a 2½-ton block. Or 16 men to move 5 tons!

While some crews were quarrying the stones, others were clearing and leveling the site of the building. A location was measured off with ropes, to form straight lines and squares. Trueness of angles could be checked by diagonals. For leveling, a long narrow trough of molded clay, holding water, served as efficiently as a modern spirit level.

It is not known exactly how the Egyptians found true north so accurately to orient their constructions. Without going into details, it is possible that they used a simple version of an artificial horizon. The Egyptians knew and used plumb bobs and were efficient enough mathematicians to do this.

As the pyramid rose, the builders raised an earthen mound on all sides of it. They hauled up the stones over long ramps; remains of such ramps have been discovered. Probably the workmen spread mud on the stones to slide one over another. As each course was laid, the mound and ramp were raised to a higher level. When the construction job was completed, all the earth was hauled away.

Contrary to popular belief, the joints between the stones were only coarsely fitted together. Probably the stone blocks were lined up on the ground and roughly trimmed to fit one another, before being hauled up the ramp and pushed into place. Evidence shows the blocks were often numbered to indicate their position and location within the structure.

Obviously, the ancient builders—without mechanical support—had to add to the number of men used to increase power. But men are bulky, and large numbers are difficult to apply at one time in a small or restricted space. They must pull, or work, in unison to be efficient—which is difficult. Equally important, they require care, housing and feeding.

Thus, Herodotus' estimate of manpower is greatly exaggerated. His figures would amount to over two million man-years of labor. The pyramids were built in a fraction of that time.

It is probable that the Pharaoh maintained a small permanent staff of skilled workmen the year around. The ruined quarters, or barracks, for such a staff have been found, accommodating about four thousand men.

Of course the Pharaoh had the power to conscript ten thousand or more peasants—or whatever number he needed. The peasants could help during the annual season when the Nile flooded—at such a time they would have been idle anyway. It is believed that this "conscription" was a form of government make-work project to keep the peasants busy and to stimulate the economy. It is not probable that much slavery was used. It would appear that forced labor was a tax-gathering effort.

Nile boatmen were also drafted to ferry slabs of limestone and granite, in boats and rafts, across or down the river from more distant quarries.

Because of the grandeur of the pyramids, it is easy to overlook the Egyptian canals—another major concern of the Pharaohs. Canals were needed to control the high rises or low ebbs of the Nile and to irrigate farm plots.

Sesostris (Senusert) III, a Pharaoh of the twenty-first century B.C., was one of the most active canal and irrigation system builders. He also constructed dams. The Egyptians were familiar with marine construction. Much later, after Sesostris III, a canal was built by Necho II (or Niku) to connect the Red Sea with the Mediterranean; this was about 600 B.C.

Much has already been written about the huge obelisks, weighing scores of tons, raised erect by the Egyptians. We know almost exactly how this was done, because a gang of Egyptian workmen recently used a very ancient method to erect a gigantic statue in a park—

The monument was hauled up a ramp constructed of earth. The dirt was dug away under the butt until the obelisk tipped upward to a 45-degree angle. When the lowest edge of the monument rested in line in a groove along the upper edge of the sunken pedestal, the laborers hauled the great stone shaft upright with ropes and shears. Shears are a pair of long heavy timbers, lashed or pegged together, to form an inverted V. A stout rope was passed over the apex for hoisting. In its way, this served as a crude pulley.

Actually, the true secrets of the ancient builders are clear. They skillfully used the fundamental instruments they had: plumb bob, primitive level gauge, heavy rope, sled, roller, lever, and shears. Cutting and planing tools were simply harder stones used on softer ones. They also had some knowledge of quarry work, including fracture lines in rocks.

Next, the ancient rulers had access to unlimited manpower—if they needed it. Equally important, the king, emperor or pharaoh had the necessary organization to command—and support—his labor force. If logistics are correct, army commanders have discovered that for each soldier on a fighting front, four additional men are needed to support him from behind the lines. If 10,000 laborers are building a great pyramid or other huge structure, then an additional 40,000 are needed for transport, supplies of all kinds, as well as food, clothing and other personal needs. Possibly, in ancient days, even more men were needed for this type of support. The old Chinese emperors, you will recall, established farms, planted and reaped crops along the construction routes to ensure sufficient food supplies.

Finally, the third important element was unlimited time. No deadline was established for completion of a project. If it took a year, ten years, or a lifetime, the work continued.

What the old Egyptians learned about quarrying, shaping, and moving heavy stones became part of the whole ancient world's general fund of technical knowledge around the Mediterranean. Later, the old Greeks inherited this knowledge and know-how, too.

Although the Egyptians surpassed all other preclassical people in the art of building with stone, in Mesopotamia (Land Between Rivers) the people were also fine engineers. Great civilizations rose and fell—Sumer and Babylon in particular. Mesopotamia lacked stone and wood, so the Mesopotamians built with brick; they used cane reeds, tied in bundles or woven into mats, as reinforcing material for canals, and asphalt from natural oil wells for both waterproofing and mortar. Bricks were made of clay mixed with straw, then sundried. Because of scarcity of fuel, only bricks used in public buildings were baked in kilns.

By 605 B.C., Babylon was the greatest city in the world. It was about one-and-a-half miles long and not quite a mile wide. The Euphrates River ran diagonally through the city, and moats carried water throughout it—forming a number of

triangular shaped islands. Babylon boasted of a main processional street paved with flagstones of lime. An outer wall, 20–
25-feet thick and possibly as high as 75 feet, with towers
spaced at intervals, encircled the city.

However, paving in ancient cities seems to have been limited
to ceremonial and processional ways. Not until Roman times
were roads paved between cities.

The Babylonians knew how to build stone barrel vaults as
well as true arches. Oddly enough, Babylon had a legend of an
underground tunnel beneath the Euphrates; this reminds me of
the underwater tunnel in Nan Madol.

The first temples in Sumer may have been built as early as
3500 B.C. Made of brick, they were designed in stark, simple
lines. To make them more impressive, the temples were later
raised on flat-topped pyramid platforms, also of brick—zig-
gurats.

City dwellers lived in rectangular-shaped houses constructed
of brick; a house might be whitewashed or, if the owner was
rich enough, coated with plaster. The rooms formed a hollow
square with doors and windows facing an open court or garden. Larger houses were often two stories high. The outside
of a house, except for the front door, presented a blank wall to
the outside world.

Because of the intense summer heat in Mesopotamia, this
arrangement of rooms permitted ventilation. Also, the layout
offered more protection against burglars, in addition to greater
privacy against government spying and tax collectors. Some
cities were laid out in a partly regular pattern, but none had
sewers, or garbage and trash collection.

This type of house and city planning may have been
adopted and improved on in the Indus Valley. Some Egyptian,
Phoenician, and Greek cities also adopted it.

Phillipe Diolé, Director of Undersea Archaeological Research for the French National Museums, says: "Before Cyrus
the Great [600?–529 B.C.] the destinies of Sumer and Mohenjo
Daro had been so closely intermingled, that it is impossible
for us now to be certain which of the two civilizations gave
birth to the other."

As we know, trading posts had long existed between Sumer

and the Indus Valley. India was important in world trade; after all, it was the country of incense, the spice road, and the storehouse of aromatics. Certainly there must have been a cultural exchange between the two countries, as well as trade.

The unique stone construction of Nan Madol has sent me searching for a link between this tiny dot of land in the East Pacific and a civilization, as yet unidentified, that had the ability and know-how to build the city. As Rome was not built in a day, neither was Nan Madol. The Romans, however, had a long history of expert building in stone; the Ponapeans did not.

A thousand years after the fall of the Indus civilization, stone construction appeared in India. Ancient stone dwellings ranged one above the other on small terraces. Construction included thick walls of undressed, but carefully laid stone slabs. These date back at least to the Buddhist period, 563?–483? B.C. Some dwellings had half a dozen or more rooms adjoining a heavy, square, keeplike tower. The ancient Indians of this period were evidently aware of cement. They used a hard cementlike plaster to cover the domes on the outside of monuments such as stupas.

When Alexander invaded India, he was opposed by a force of 2,000 cavalry, more than 30,000 infantry, and 30 elephants. This indicates that the Indians were hardly unorganized or uncivilized. Such a large army requires careful planning, good routes of supply, and a strong central authority. The Indus River flows from northwest India two thousand miles into the Arabian Sea, and Alexander had to fight almost every foot of his way.

Experts explain that stone structures are developed in imitation of existing wooden houses and buildings. If this were true, where did the model exist for Nan Madol? The Ponapeans and other Micronesians did not construct wooden houses and buildings. They restricted themselves almost entirely to brush-cane-thatched huts, meeting houses, and similar large buildings on ceremonial sites.

Ancient Ponapean legends say that Nan Madol was built by a black people, by "evil" black dwarfs, by two magicians who chanted magical formulas, by (unidentified) strangers who came out of the sea from the east, and so on—and on!—giving the reader a wide range of choice. The simple truth is that the Ponapeans have no idea or memory or oral history that accounts for the construction of the great city.

Some experts assert that Micronesians did, indeed, build the city in a period of creative energy. They may be correct, but possibly not *very* when they point out the huge megalithic constructions in Europe. Ponape is nearly as isolated a spot on earth as it is possible to find; the megalithic builders were in contact, even if indirectly, with the traditions of the ancient Mediterranean engineers.

In Europe, megalithic construction around 2000–1500 B.C., in the main, is found in the British Isles, France and the western Mediterranean. Literally thousands of them were erected.

Megaliths are great undressed rough stones used in groups to erect chamber tombs; in ceremonial rows, enclosures, and in monuments. A *menhir* is a single great standing stone. In Cyclopean architecture, large slabs are placed one on top of another.

In Stonehenge, the most famous of these ancient structures, the largest megalith was 29 feet, 8 inches long. The great menhir, in Locmariaquer in southern Brittany, when intact, was 65 feet long. A capstone of the Mt. Browne dolmen, in County Carlow, Ireland, weighs about a hundred tons.

The famous "blue" stones of Stonehenge came from Pembrokeshire—140 miles as the crow flies, to Salisbury Plain. Various routes have been suggested for the stones' transportation. All land routes crossing the Severn near Gloucester are about 180 miles by sea to the Mendips and then by land for another 150 miles. A long sea route around Cornwall and up the Hampshire Avon is nearly 400 miles. No one knows which route was used.

In Japan, a megalithic tomb of Ishibutai has two capstones, each weighing between 60 and 70 tons. A professor at the University of Kyoto made calculations on how it was constructed: the stones were dragged on sledges and rollers up earthen banks—planes up which dragging could take place. The raising of stones was accomplished by means of radiating levers and weights. Professor Takahashi estimated that it took 300–400 men one year to do this.

Alexander Keiller, in 1934, experimented in raising a fallen megalith of average size. (What is an average-sized megalith?) Anyhow, Mr. Keiller used one skilled foreman and twelve unskilled workmen without tools. They put up the stone in five days.

Megaliths and associated architecture are subjects in themselves. I mention them here only to show that the ancient men of the Mediterranean and western Europe were long familiar with erecting huge stone monuments and moving extremely heavy weights, some for long distances. (True in Asia, too.)

Clues have already been uncovered as to *how* vast heavy amounts of material were handled. The questions now remaining are by *whom* and *when* similar material was moved, in a place halfway around the world from the Mediterranean, to build Nan Madol.

chapter
10

From very early times, ancient man was able to build effectively with great stones. If stone was not available, then he used other materials, such as brick and wood. What we can be certain of, in Europe and the Mediterranean, he utilized earthen ramps to raise the height of his building. In Nan Madol this is not certain at all. The builders of Nan Madol began their construction on the sea bottom in shallow waters. The Mediterranean engineers proved they could transport very heavy weights by boats and rafts. So, it is not impossible that the stone "logs" of Nan Madol were transported in the same manner. When beginning construction of an artificial island, a heavy stone could be floated to an almost exact position, then unloaded in place. As described before, the logs rose in a cribbing pattern.

However, once the logs rose above the surface of the water, the problem of raising the heavy logs to a greater height had to be faced. The Ponapeans were not in a position to use earthen ramps. They were building in the midst of water, and earth deposited to build a ramp would wash away almost as fast as it was deposited. One explanation might be that the builders used small coral stones for ramps, then upon completion utilized the coral rubble to fill in between the walls. This theory may be acceptable so far as it goes, but another problem arises immediately. As we know, the individual islands rose about six feet above the surface. Then, the building of the structures began. They were usually set back a short distance from the edges of the islands. Little space remained to erect ramps with a gradual incline for building walls 30 feet high, or higher.

We do not know whether the Ponapeans used rollers beneath the logs—hauling and pushing them up the incline. It is unlikely that they rolled the logs without rollers, because of the basalt's rectangular shapes. The stones could not be rolled. It is also doubtful that a type of sled, such as the Egyptian, could be used. Stone rubble was not smooth enough to be efficient. Nor in the confines of a small artificial island could a large number of workmen labor effectively.

It seems possible, therefore, that when Nan Madol was built the engineers had knowledge more advanced than is usually credited to them. I will try to find *what* knowledge this was, and *where* it came from.

The building of a large city of huge stones is entirely different from the problem of raising huge stone statues—even though there are many of them. Thor Heyerdahl in 1956 organized transport of one of the great statues on Easter Island. He erected it without any mechanical aids by what he believed to be the original technique.

He organized a team of 180 Easter Islanders who dragged a 30-ton statue from the quarry to the spot where it was to be erected. At the selected location, by levering and hauling, twelve islanders raised it to the vertical in eighteen days!

Most of the illustrations I have used have demonstrated that vast numbers of workmen are not necessary to handle great weights. A sufficient number, yes; but fewer, by far, than would be expected. Unfortunately, however, the demonstrations pointed out here, and earlier, were usually conducted on firm ground. Nan Madol presented additional problems—confined space and unstable water.

I have dug into the background of old civilizations, look-

In the background, and to the right of center, is a section of rock cribbing rising about five feet above the surface of the water. This is typical of the construction of an artificial islet. Because of the thick tropical growth covering the small island, the walls and ruins in the interior cannot be seen. To the left, huge mangrove roots are sunk deep into the channel.

ing for an important, in fact *essential*, clue that might explain Nan Madol. Perhaps I should quote Geoffrey Scott, deceased, an authority in the field of the history of architecture; he wrote: "It is [thus] the last sign of an artificial civilization when Nature takes the place of art." I know of no decoration or art of any kind existing in Nan Madol. As a construction it was stark, strict and raw. From Scott's definition, it must appear that Nan Madol did not develop over a period of time. It did not grow out of a preceding culture. It did not improve on existing foundations of civilization. It seems to be unique —strictly one of a kind!

But I do realize that *something* had to start it off.

During the last million years, human invention has progressed with glacial slowness. Men chopped with ax-heads of stone, grasped in their fists, for hundreds of thousands of years. About 100,000 years ago, however, men had probably become as intelligent as we are today—but still technology advanced at a crawl.

Anthropologists give us some reasons: primitive peoples lived a hand-to-mouth existence. They could not risk trying a new experiment. Primitive societies were very conservative. An "inventor" was likely to be considered dangerous—either as a deviationist or a practitioner of black magic. And finally, the odds against a new invention were numerically high among the small tribal bands numbering only 50 to 100 persons, counting the children.

To illustrate this, consider the number of inventions in the United States, a country famous for its inventors. In a population of 218 million people, there is only *one* patentable invention each year for every 4,500 citizens. And this under the best of conditions, where everyone is encouraged to come up with a new and practical idea—and, if successful, make a fortune!

The diffusionist theory holds that all civilization came from only a few old civilized centers. However, independent invention has, and does, take place simultaneously in different countries. What is probable is that invention contains some borrowing, and every borrowing, some invention. Where a line is drawn is a personal decision.

It is not necessary for an invention to make a journey. A man hears a rumor, a story, a bit of gossip regarding a new and useful kind of object in a foreign tribe or land. From the description, he takes the basic idea and starts working on a similar invention. His invention, when completed, may be quite different from the original.

In the vast area of Oceania were inventions available to the builders of Nan Madol, so that, by using them, they could erect the large city under the circumstances described? It is believed by some authorities that the first human occupation of Oceania (Polynesia, Melanesia and Micronesia) occurred in New Guinea during, or shortly after, the last Ice Age. At that time sea levels were lower and distances between Australia, New Guinea and other Indonesian islands were less. Primitive stone tools and charcoal used during that time, found in New Guinea, are carbon-14-dated to more than 25,000 years old.

When the melting ice of the great glaciers raised the ocean levels, distances increased. The black Melanesians became more isolated until brown-skinned peoples from Asiatic islands reached Indonesia, the Philippines and Taiwan, and continued on to New Guinea and other islands, about 4,500 years ago. The Melanesians were already settled there and they remained.

It is believed that the Polynesians arrived in small groups by various routes and remained isolated, possibly, in a home group of islands. This may have occurred in Tonga and Samoa three thousand years ago. It is doubtful, though, that they migrated through Melanesia, or they would have had contact with shell and stone money and the custom of chewing betel with lime; and they would have known the loom and pottery, which the Melanesians knew and used. Also, through intermarriage, the Polynesians would have had darker skins and acquired the "B" factor in their blood. Eventually, when they headed again into the vast Pacific, they probably pushed their way up through Micronesia.

None of the Polynesians, Micronesians or Melanesians used an arch in building, and mortar was unknown. Nor did any of them construct roofed stone buildings. The best they came up with were small subterranean chambers with single stone slabs stretching from wall to wall.

As you have discovered by now, it is difficult, without a map, to follow the routes taken by the great mixtures of all the cultural elements found in the western Pacific. Many of the top authorities do not agree among themselves, which does not make our task any easier. For our purposes, I will try to arrange a time schedule; many experts will disagree with it. I do not pretend that this schedule is entirely accurate, but it is a sort of consensus of many authorities:

500–200 B.C.	The first Indian traders appear in Malaysia.
1–400 A.D.	The ancestors of the Polynesians strike out from eastern Malaysia into the South Seas.
683 A.D.	The very well-developed state of Sri-Vijaya in Sumatra is in existence.
750–850 A.D.	The great Boro Budur Shrine is built in Java.
939 A.D.	A great stone city, Angkor Thom, in Cambodia. The more famous Angkor Wat is not built until much later—from the twelfth century on.

What this points out is that, from the seventh century on, magnificent stone constructions were being erected in the Malaysia and Indonesia areas. Knowledge and skill to work the stone in intricate plans, and to decorate the huge structures with artistic and beautiful designs are not accomplishments gained quickly. How long it might have been going on before blossoming out in all its glory, is not certain. Too, these sites are a very long way from Ponape, in Micronesia.

Sometime in the distant past, possibly around the beginning of the Christian era, or even before, knowledge of building in stone began circulating east of India into the South China Sea and beyond. It is not surprising that it took centuries for the skill and know-how to develop. The great stone cities and buildings, mentioned in our schedule, were the end result. They compare with about as much similarity to Nan Madol, however, as an expensive limousine bears to a bicycle.

E. S. C. Handy wrote:

> Just about the beginning of the Christian era, Indians, coming by sea, were founding great and enduring kingdoms in Sumatra, Java, Borneo, Cambodia and Annam ... traded with Asia Minor, Africa and Rome in the west, and also the Far East.

This certainly supports my theory, which is beginning to take shape. However, as the clues are beginning to come together, I have a feeling that *my* builders of Nan Madol antedated the Christian era. At least their origins did, if not the actual start of the building.

Languages often indicate common origins of peoples. The languages of Micronesia, Polynesia, Melanesia and Indonesia all belong to one great Austronesian family that extends as far west as Madagascar. But in Micronesia, no truly native language exists. For instance, the tongues on Saipan, Yap, Palau, Truk, Ponape, Kusaie and Majuro are all different. Some scholars believe that a few of the dialects have traces of the Japanese language. Like the Chinese, Japanese junks were often wrecked in the islands. We are told that in North America, at one time, three hundred different Indian languages were spoken.

Ainoids, an ancient basically white people, are thought to have migrated out of Asia to Oceania. The Ainoids were akin to Caucasoid people of Europe and the very old Ainu strain in Japan. Were the Ainu, conquered and dominated by the Jap invaders, responsible for blood and language traces in Micronesia? The question is not going to be answered soon.

The trail is becoming complicated, especially when the Veddoids are taken into consideration. The Veddoids were also an ancient people, related to the Vedda people of Ceylon and South India. They migrated to Australia and western Melanesia. Taller and lighter in color than the very early Negrito settlers, the Veddoids intermixed to form the present-day Melanesian population.

These peoples, and others, are all part of the problem when I try to find a link to the Ponapeans. Most of the time, digging in the past, I come to a dead end. Or, at best, I find no proof, even hypothetical, to explain the unexpected engineering achievement culminating in raising Nan Madol.

From time to time, I have stumbled on the long trail of the Polynesians. No discussion of Oceania is complete without an understanding of the important part these people played in its settlement. At various times the Polynesians were in contact with the Micronesians. For how long, no one is quite sure.

Some authorities believe the early ancestors of the Polynesians evolved on the coasts of southern and southeast Asia. They claim that a relationship existed between the Chinese Bronze Age culture and the far-eastern islands of the Pacific—the Marquesas group. The Marquesas, settled by the Polynesians, have offered up types of coral files, stone adzes, and a unique fishbook not found elsewhere but indicating a past connection with Chinese influence. Ancient campfires of Ha'atuatura have been carbon-dated to around 120 B.C. This date is after the western Polynesian islands were settled.

The first groups of Polynesian settlers sailed out to form independent colonies. They arrived fully prepared, bringing with them pigs, dogs, oats, coconuts, sweet-potato sets, cuttings from breadfruit trees, and yam plantings. Possibly two or three hundred persons, including women and children, were in the exploring party. As is known, the Polynesians could travel fantastic distances in their great catamaran canoes lashed together to provide deck space and living quarters.

The Polynesians' appearance in Oceania and the routes they took are sometimes explained as originating with the Shang dynasty (1766–1122 B.C.), a Bronze Age culture. Along with other peoples, the Polynesians were forced out of their homelands. Over a number of years, they moved out in small groups or social units. Coming down the Malay peninsula, some settled in Indonesia. The Marianas had already been settled and possibly parts of the Philippines. They pushed on to Fiji and New Caledonia. From Fiji they pressed on to the Tongan group and then into western Polynesia.

To reach the Marquesas, they sailed a distance of 1,600 miles, bypassing many large land groups on the way. The colonists probably followed equatorial countercurrents or the countertrades that blow periodically through the Pacific from the northwest.

Cultural objects indicate that the Polynesians came from a volcanic island in western Polynesia similar to some of the Melanesian islands—possibly Tonga, with dates going back to 1140 B.C.

This does not mean that all the Polynesians sailed this route, anymore than that all the Polynesians ended up in the Marquesas. It does indicate that some Polynesians had reached the Marquesas as early as 120 B.C. For our purposes, this is an important date to remember. It is also important to recall that other Polynesians sailed north through Micronesia and settled two islands in the same region as Ponape.

By 400 A.D., according to possible carbon-14 dates, the Polynesians had reached Easter Island—their easternmost island. It is also the most isolated.

A confusing point about these dates is that they all seem so old, covering such long spans of time. One indication they have in common is that they point back to the beginnings of the Christian era, and well beyond. This may become more important when I try to determine the founding of Nan Madol.

chapter
11

I pause momentarily for what a television announcer might call a station break. In this search, we—you and I—are indebted to the archaeologists, anthropologists, historians and all the other scientists who have brought to light the bits of facts and figures that are being used in the search. I've picked up a piece here and another piece there and tried to fit them together, hoping that eventually they will form enough of a picture to answer my questions.

Too often, as you have seen, a trail will lead to no conclusion, but along the way we glean a new, and often tiny, bit of information. Like a jigsaw puzzle, if one piece does not exactly fit the next, we put it aside and hope to be able to use it later.

So I will keep at it. Now I have more information to help me than when I started.

Just how much of an agricultural system the ancient Ponapeans developed is unknown; because of the abundance of rainfall, irrigation was not necessary. Harvests from the sea were undoubtedly important. If Nan Madol was a city, the hub of a maritime empire, it would indeed be an advanced conception in its place and time.

To construct an agricultural civilization and to conceive the idea of a civilization based upon the sea, are linked endeavors that demand patience, dedication and continuity. Did, or could, this happen to the Ponapeans?

Ashley Montagu wrote:

> The earth is a very large place and upon its surface men have lived in small groups, isolated from one another for long periods of time, until the very recent period . . . under conditions of isolation and random mutation—all mutation being random—every isolated group, no matter how like other groups it originally was, would more or less rapidly become distinguished from all other groups by virtue of the differences in the mutations which would arise in each group.

However the above quotation is defined, I simply do not believe that mutation is the explanation for the tremendous effort and imagination required to build Nan Madol.

Nan Madol was and is an achievement worthy of a highly civilized state. As we have seen, though, it is far from a city of beauty or artistic merit. It is a stark, barbaric construction of monumental proportions. One might theorize that, although its builders knew how to move and erect great stones, they did not know how to work them. Reliefs, sculptures and decorations were beyond their skills.

Carving stone images or statues is a creative art. Not even small portable stone images have been found in Micronesia or in central or western Polynesia. Dr. Buck has written that "The time spent in the atolls of Micronesia would be long enough to erase memory of former arts."

Far to the east, in Oceania, some stone images did appear, but these were of a much later date. They were made in the Marquesas, Raivavae, Hawaii and New Zealand. These were small, and often crude, little images called *tikis*. The god Tiki was always shown in much the same way—almost an embryonic form with hands clutching its belly. The face was depicted with goggle eyes, open mouth and protruding tongue. Usually they are small—not more than three and a half feet tall.

102

Also in the Marquesas, crude, rude scratches on rocks—petro-glyphs—have been found. These are stick figures of men, pigs, dogs and fish, and they date from very early days—possibly two thousand years ago—and precede the statues by many centuries. Some authorities believe the stone sculptures came much later—only a century or two before the arrival of the Europeans.

Thor Heyerdahl writes of an interesting discovery he made when he first visited the island of Fatu Hiva in the Marquesas. In the forest a giant tree had fallen; it was very large and very old. In falling, the tree's roots had pulled away to disclose two huge stone slabs. The slabs were covered with petroglyphs. One incised drawing was of a fish, six feet in length, complete with head, tail, and fins. It was also covered with cup-shaped depressions and symbolic signs. The designs were sun symbols —a dot, surrounded by concentric rings. He also found draw-ings of masks with eyes.

Heyerdahl cleared away more of the underbrush and made additional discoveries. Also on the rock were complete human figures with hooked arms and legs, *a turtle,* and a *crescent-shaped ship with a curved bottom, a high bow and stern, a double mast and rows of oars.* The islanders of the Marquesas group had never sailed in anything other than dugout canoes and flat rafts.

In another location, high up in the hills overlooking a valley, Heyerdahl made a completely fascinating discovery. What he found was "a large slab sculptured into a *turtle.* This was probably an altar for sacrifice."

Always staring at us from the pages of history, is Easter Island and its famous stone heads. These huge statues required skilled labor directed by artistic talent in addition to long ex-perience and a sense of mathematical exactness. Large numbers of laborers had to be organized and supervised by men fa-miliar with engineering problems and the handling of Cyclo-pean monoliths. Some of the statues were over 30 feet long and weighed as much as 50 tons.

These huge stone-head sculptures appeared somewhat late in Oceanic history. The Polynesians' own traditions, corrobo-rated to some degree by archaeology, say they moved into

Polynesia from Indonesia (they mention Java in particular) within the last one thousand years and reached Easter Island around 1300 A.D. Others say it was 1150 A.D. It is interesting to speculate why the new migrants stayed on Easter Island—a barren, treeless place. Originally, the newcomers were seamen; but the treeless island had no materials for shipbuilding. Eventually, the old boats wore out; the islanders were stuck there!

When the Easter Islanders turned to sculpturing, they had available a reddish sandstone, more easily workable than most stones, as well as a gray, fine-grained and polishable *tuff*. They carried memories of stone carving from the Marquesas to their new home and developed their own highly individual pattern. Dr. Hibben believes, however, they came from the Solomon group.

Necker Island in the Hawaii group also has small stone statues. These are crudely sculptured from hard basalt, similar to the tikis found in the Marquesas, but are very small, ranging in size from eight inches to eighteen inches.

Far more sculpture and a greater variety are found in Melanesia. Here is found a form of "collage sculpture," which includes bark cloth, raffia, reeds, bone, shell and wood. Unfortunately, the material disintegrates and rots quickly.

The Melanesians also used a three-pronged motif of an unknown origin and significance. It looks very much like a variation of the old Greek god Neptune's trident.

Mention of a trident, and I run again into the ubiquitous Greeks. Even before the discovery and use of mortar, men could build a good solid wall of small stones that stood up to the weather for years. However, an enemy could easily pry out a few stones and the wall would collapse.

As a matter of necessity, the old engineers began to construct walls of very large stones, roughly trimming and fitting them together. The sheer weight of the huge stones prevented the foe from pulling them out—especially if the defenders atop the wall were raining down missiles. Such walls were called "Cyclopean" by the ancient Greeks because when they saw the ruins, centuries old, they thought the walls were built by the mythical one-eyed giant, Cyclops.

Cyclopean walls have been built for eons. To build one, however, required great labor and some engineering knowledge.

Nan Madol is a Cyclopean city, crude but effective. It stands alone in Oceania, although other examples of stone construction are found elsewhere. Polynesians on their easternmost islands showed skill in stone shaping with intricate forms of jointing and mortising. Their achievements were limited to uprights, stone statues, walls and large raised platforms. The Polynesians elevated stone platforms that sometimes resembled low truncated pyramids and were used for religious purposes. Occasionally these were "stepped" pyramids, but they were low structures covering small to large areas. Probably none was over forty feet high; some were as low as three feet.

An expedition to Nuku Hiva, an island in the Marquesas group, revealed big stone platforms, terraces and dancing areas. This type of construction started early in the 1500s and continued through the 1860s. The Spaniards reported seeing stone platforms in 1596, so the constructions date back at least that far, and probably further. In a historical perspective, these are recent dates.

Like the Ponapeans, the Polynesians had no idea of a keystone to hold an arch in position, thus permitting roofed constructions. To some observers it might appear that the Polynesians did not improve very much on the old Nan Madol technique of building, or even that the Polynesians did not know of it.

But we cannot be sure. In Micronesia, in the Marshall Islands, there are certain cultural similarities between the Micronesians and the Polynesians, and these similarities grow stronger the farther eastward they go, to the last tiny coral atolls in the Gilbert Islands. In trying to sort out similarities, it is helpful to remember that the Micronesian part of the Pacific equals the whole north Atlantic Ocean in size. Distances are so vast that time becomes relative. In the tribes, each family occasionally had ten children with corresponding increases of grandchildren. But it still required centuries before colonists could spread themselves to establish new kingdoms over the vast spreads of the archipelagoes.

If, as it is sometimes claimed, it required 20,000–50,000

workmen to build Nan Madol over a thousand years ago, it would have required untold numbers of generations to reach the population required. Earlier, we have seen that it probably did not require such a fantastic work force.

My real problem is that I do not *really* know when Ponape was first settled. The present Ponapeans are certainly not the descendants of the original settlers, who, possibly from earliest prehistoric days, were black Melanesians. The modern existing legends of "black dwarfs" substantiate this to a degree; also, we know it was once invaded and conquered by warriors from Kusaie long after Nan Madol had been built.

Dates in Oceania are confusing and conflicting. For instance, Easter Island natives claim to be able to count back fifty-seven generations, from the end of the last century. This would give a date of their settlement on the island (1,425 years ago), at approximately 450 A.D. Experts, however, fix the date of their arrival between 1150 and 1300 A.D. Another example is the Hawaiians, who give a disputed date of arrival at approximately 800 A.D. This is interesting because some authorities believe the Hawaiians arrived from Tonga and Samoa—islands possibly settled about 1000 A.D. Percy Smith, on the other hand, believes the Polynesians reached Samoa around 450 A.D. It simply goes on and on.

Pottery, as noted before, is lacking in almost all of Oceania. This is unfortunate, an archaeological calamity, as pottery shards are important guides to time. They can be carbon-dated to indicate levels of skill and art as well as possible connections between different societies. If there is *any* pottery, it should certainly be examined more closely.

That is the rub! There is not much to examine. Prehistoric fragments of pottery have been found on Guam, Saipan, Rota and Tinian in the Mariana Islands. As the gull flies, Guam is roughly a thousand miles from Ponape. Possibly, this is the closest that pottery has been found to Nan Madol, until quite recently. Dr. Kenneth P. Emory told me that some pottery has been discovered in that area, but it has not yet been dated, and no authentic report on the finds has been made.

The pottery found in parts of Melanesia, but also in Samoa and Tonga, is of a prehistoric decorated type named *Lapita*.

Tonga is generally recognized as the oldest occupied island in Polynesia, and the pottery found there is carbon-dated as of 1140 B.C. The samples found on Samoa are not so old; they are dated as of about 500 B.C. Nevertheless, pottery had existed so far in the past that the natives had no knowledge of it. The same was true of the Marquesans, who did not even have a word in their vocabulary for pottery.

The first pottery was crude and inferior. Then there was simply no pottery at all. This happened on other islands—the art of pottery making just died out. The same was true in Melanesia on Banks Island, Pentecost and Malekula. Apparently, as I have noted earlier, the lack of good pottery clay and the presence of natural containers such as coconuts and bottle gourds made pottery no longer a necessity.

Much the same happened with weaving. The loom was known in Indonesia. The earliest fabrics belong to the ancient Mohenjo-Daro civilization in the Indus Valley. But use of a loom was almost unknown in Micronesia, Polynesia and Melanesia. Possibly this is explained by the absence of cotton in those areas. There were exceptions. Some cotton, of poor primitive type, did grow occasionally on a few islands. This wild cotton was of an extremely low quality. Good domestic cotton reached China only about 700 A.D., and it never spread into the Pacific farther than Java and the Philippines. Some evidence indicates that the loom appeared sporadically in Melanesia and Micronesia, and passed through the Carolines.

The absence of good-quality cotton made bark cloth (tapa) more desirable and easier to make. Thus bark cloth took the place of other fabrics. It, too, quickly and easily deteriorates. What bits and pieces still exist are of too recent an origin to mean much. Compare this with the ancient Egyptian mummy wrapping, in museums, which are thousands of years old.

Another lack in Oceania that was discussed earlier is the absence of metal tools and weapons. R. C. Majumdar, author of *Ancient Indian Colonies in the Far East*, has written that iron lance points, two thousand years old, have been found in prehistoric graves in Java together with short iron swords. These artifacts are ascribed to people or peoples who settled in Java many centuries before the Hindu colonization.

It is logical to reason that if the ores for making metal weapons and tools are lacking, then whoever possessed this equipment must have carried the finished products with them. Scarcely any metal ore is found anywhere in the Pacific. The Carolines, including Ponape, have traces of limonite, a yellowish iron ore, but the resources are in such a limited quantity as to be useless. Iron and copper, also in very small quantities have been found on Yap, an island 1,200 miles distant from Ponape. Sufficient to say, no metal weapon or tool has ever been found in Nan Madol. Or, for that matter, anywhere in Micronesia and Polynesia.

A direct contrast, of course, to Europe and the Middle East, where archaeologists have discovered copper objects existing as early as 4500 B.C. By 3000 B.C., copper had displaced stone for tools and weapons. In Tell Asmar, an iron dagger handle has been dated to around 2700 B.C. It was almost another thousand years, however, before iron became widely used.

The lack of metal objects, throughout Micronesia, makes accurate dating very difficult, especially when no written records exist. In the West, surviving cuneiform clay tablets, Egyptian hieroglyphic inscriptions and demotic writings, Greek and other Mediterranean records and manuscripts, and our own Bible have all contributed some point of reference from which archaeologists and historians could work.

This is all the more mystifying because, W. D. Alexander, in his book *The Origin of the Polynesian Race,* wrote:

> We learn from Javan traditions that from and after 300 B.C., several successive waves of emigration from Eastern India entered the Archipelago, bringing with them the Hindu civilization of that period, the Buddhist religion, and the art of writing; besides a large number of Sanskrit terms of which no trace is found in the Polynesian dialect.

And no traces of Buddhism have been found in Micronesia, either.

At the time of which Professor Alexander writes, Japan and China had built great trading empires along the coastal areas of Asia, and these extended to India and Java. Chinese annals describe these contacts in the Indonesian Archipelago from the Han period—206 B.C.—and later. What is more remarkable is that in the second century A.D., Ptolemy (Book VII) wrote that the Romans of his day had detailed knowledge of the coasts of India, Indochina, Sumatra, Java and China.

Why, with all the contacts offered by the advanced civilizations of those ages, did so few cultural refinements seep through to the peoples of Micronesia? One explanation, in part, might be the tremendous distances involved—the great expanses of ocean and the very small lands, islands, within them. Another might be, as was mentioned before, the possibility that skills once known and utilized were forgotten over generations of time spent on atolls and tiny islands, where such skills were no longer needed, or because of lack of raw materials.

chapter
12

Police authorities have told me that often what is *missing* in a case they are working on is as important as what they find. In my detection work to solve the mystery of Nan Madol, perhaps I should pause here, about halfway through the case, and list what I do know so far, and what is missing. By "missing" is meant skills, artifacts, arts, et cetera, that Ponapeans, and Micronesians generally, might be expected to have in common with other societies advanced enough to have built Nan Madol.

First, we know that Ponape, with its great city, is extremely isolated; no trade routes or sea paths exist within thousands of miles of it.

At its zenith, the island (including the surrounding smaller ones) could not have supported a large population. As a guess, based on natural resources, possibly around 20,000 persons.

The city is built in a most primitive fashion, but building it still required a tremendous effort of labor and engineering know-how. The techniques required to erect a city of this kind had been well known to other civilizations for thousands of years; where, how, or when the Ponapeans received that technical knowledge I simply do not know. I also believe that the engineers of Nan Madol had somewhat better technical knowledge than did the previous Cyclopean engineers of far earlier constructions. To build a canal city on water presented some new and different problems.

Nan Madol practiced religion based on sacred turtle worship. We have few details of it. India, in particular, and ancient Europe also, included the turtle, or tortoise, to some degree in religious practice. That even a tenuous connection exists between these civilizations and Nan Madol is not certain.

The old Micronesians, including the Ponapeans, were competent seamen, but not so expert as the later Polynesians.

Ponape, as well as Nan Madol, was governed by kings. An aristocracy, a nobility, a priesthood and commoners made up the social structure. Possibly a slave portion of the population existed, too. Although not a common practice, slavery is found throughout areas of old Oceania.

The Ponapeans held a reputation as extraordinarily brave warriors. Their weapons deserve a closer examination.

Although basalt rock formations are found on other islands of volcanic origin, the basalt-crystal formations are peculiar to Ponape.

Experts disagree regarding the dates when Nan Madol was founded. These dates vary between 700 and 1285 A.D.; some even so late as the 1500s. Others believe it may go back to the beginning of the Christian era. I am starting to lean toward this earlier date.

The city of Nan Madol has no art, decorations, statues or sculptures of any kind. Nor did it have metal tools or weapons.

The canals, when constructed, were not so deep or wide as to accommodate ships other than canoes.

The Ponapeans, when first visited by Europeans, had no memory of when the city was built, or how it was erected, except for vague legends based on magical solutions.

Present Ponapeans and their preceding generations have demonstrated no skill, or even *interest,* in any kind of stone construction. A small island, Kusaie, about three hundred miles away, has similar, but smaller, ruins. No other construction remotely resembling Nan Madol is found anywhere in Oceania.

The Ponapeans have a legend that their island was originally inhabited by a race of black people. Another legend about "evil black dwarfs" also exists; these may be evil spirits and demons living in the mountains. There are still place names relating to these dwarfs today.

An underwater tunnel of sorts exists from near the center of Nan Madol to beyond the sea walls.

The ruins of the city display no signs of disaster from earthquakes. The havoc is from time, tropical jungle and storms.

No reports from earliest explorers contain references to Nan Madol. Knowledge regarding it begins early in the nineteenth century.

The "missing" clues are commonplace objects I would expect to find, but do not. This is true not only of Ponape and Micronesia, but also of Polynesia.

The Ponapeans never had a plow. Planting consisted of poking a hole in the ground with a stick and dropping a seed in it. They did not have a rake either.

They never had metal tools or weapons. Instead, they used stone or shell knives, spear points and stone-edged war clubs.

The use of a wheel was unknown, although the wheel first appeared in Sumer around 3000 B.C. and was used in the Indus Valley at a somewhat later date.

No domestic dray animals, such as horses, asses, bullocks. What they had, as mentioned, were pigs, dogs, chickens and rats.

In general, Oceania and the Old World had no food plants in common. In some cases where similar plants are found, they belong to different species.

The people had no knowledge of money, coins, or exchange tokens. Yap is an exception, as will be described later. Exchange took place through barter.

In their early contacts with Westerners, the peoples of Oceania had no hereditary immunity to Old World diseases; no epidemic diseases in common.

It is certain that they had no writing. At least not in

Ponape; and *if* it did exist, it was only in a few widely scattered places.

Finally, they lacked bellows for any kind of metalworking, as well as metal itself. No pottery wheel or pottery. No glazing. No kiln-dried bricks. And no stringed instruments.

These simple everyday objects had all been known for centuries, in some instances for thousands of years, yet—somehow—they never reached Oceania. If they did become known, then eventually the knowledge was lost.

One can understand the absence of livestock. Animals the size of horses and bullocks are too large to take on long voyages, even in pontoon-decked canoes. They would also require reserves of feed for an extended trip. The idea of a wheel, however, is simple to carry in one's head. A small two-wheeled cart can be pulled by one person and is an extremely handy article to have available.

The lack of money, coins, can be attributed to the scarcity of metals—which, in turn, might explain the absence of bellows. But our own North American Indians developed their own medium of exchange—wampum—for purposes of trade. Other primitive people worked out other devices.

The natural climate of Ponape promotes the exceptionally easy growing of food. Even a forked or pronged stick, for digging, hoeing and plowing, is an advance over a straight stick. Apparently, however, it was never invented or adopted.

It is doubtful that primitive, glazed, kiln-dried bricks would long weather the heavy rains of Ponape. So, as with pottery and the loom, it might have become a useless skill, eventually to be forgotten.

Although stringed instruments have never been found in Oceania, lack of materials, again, might explain their absence. Gut, horn and metal were not available. Other instruments were developed, however—a nose flute and drum.

It must be remembered in searching further, that, with a few exceptions, the lack of the most common primitive inventions does not prove that they never existed; what it might indicate is the possibility that for one reason or another they were never used.

The legend of the black dwarfs is not only interesting, it is a recurring one found throughout other areas of Oceania. In the Malay Peninsula, and in the adjoining Andaman Islands, true pygmy Negritos are found among the other populations.

According to ethnologists there are two main branches of the Negroid race—one in Africa, the other in Melanesia. Both are black. In the African branch, the hair is short and kinky; in the Melanesian, the hair is frizzy and grows into a heavy mop. The biggest difference in their features is in their noses. The African's is short, wide and flat. The Melanesian's is large and hooked.

Anthropologists believe that these small Negritos were the earliest inhabitants of Melanesia, but that a second group of Negroids, who were larger and more aggressive, arrived and blended in with them to become the aboriginal inhabitants of most of southeast Asia. Later, this black population was dislodged, in great measure, by invasions of more advanced peoples of a Mongoloid type.

Perhaps as long ago as 15,000 years these Asian Negroids started moving out to the islands of Melanesia. Others headed northward into Micronesia. This theory also helps to explain the presence of the Proto-Negroid race in Australia, Tasmania, New Guinea and the Philippines, as well as their influence in Micronesia.

The Melanesians apparently never were good seafarers and explorers. Yet, in one way or another, they were able to migrate over vast distances. When the Polynesians reached Hawaii, the blacks were already there. The Hawaiians enslaved them and called them *Menehune*. Occasionally, the Menehune used bows and arrows—uncommon weapons throughout Micronesia and Melanesia—and they lived on fruit. At that time and until the arrival of the Polynesians no animals inhabited the islands. These aboriginal blacks of short build later escaped to hide in the mountains.

On Ponape, the dwarf Negritos were called *Chokalai*. Ponapean legends credit the building of Nan Madol to the blacks. F. W. Christian in 1899, in his book *The Caroline Islands*, wrote: "The stone buildings of Nanmatal [*sic*] were erected by a race preceding the present inhabitants of Po-

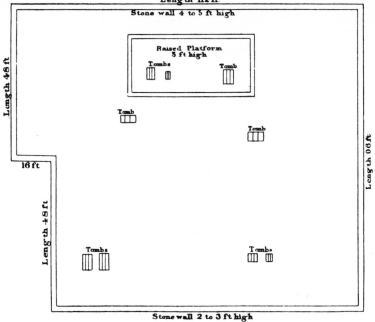

Stone wall 4 to 5 ft high

Raised Platform
5 ft high

Tombs   Tomb

Length 48 ft

Tomb

Tomb

Length 06 ft

16 ft

Length 48 ft

Tombs   Tombs

Stone wall 2 to 3 ft high

GRAVES OF THE "LITTLE PEOPLE"

*A sketch of the graveyard of "the Little People." Referred to as
"evil black dwarfs" by the Ponapeans, this race was long thought
to be legendary; however, it is probable that they were the original
inhabitants of the island. Only a few shreds of bone—and no
artifacts—were ever recovered from this burial site.* (DRAWING BY
F. W. CHRISTIAN, FROM HIS BOOK *The Caroline Islands*)

nape. . . . The builders of Nanmatal belonged to the black race
and the Ponapeans are a mixed race." Christian refers to the
legends of the dwarfs or "little folk": "These, according to
Ponapean tradition, were the little dwarfish folk who dwelt
in the land before the coming of Kona and Li-ot, the giants
and the cannibals." He explains the dwarfs were dark of skin
and flat-nosed, and continues: "They are believed still to
haunt the dark recesses of the forest, and to be very malig-
nant and revengeful."

R. Linton wrote in 1926 (*Ethnology of Polynesia and Micronesia*): "The Ponapeans had a tradition of a race of dwarf,
black aborigines who used a bow in war." (Author's Note:
I still heard this reference to "evil black dwarfs" among the
Ponapeans.)

115

Around 1900, Christian located a small graveyard of "the little people" on Ponape. It was situated in a dell called *Ponial*. It consisted only of some very crude stone vaults. (See illustration, page 115.) According to Christian, nothing was left; all the bones had disintegrated, or were gone.

Two facts gleaned about "the little people" may be important clues: first, they were not unfamiliar with building in stone, even if the work was crude; second, they used bows and arrows, weapons unknown throughout the rest of Micronesia and Polynesia.

Bows and arrows have long been known to man. The first ones are traced back ten thousand years to Spain, during the Neolithic Age. They may even be older. This kind of weapon has been found not only in Europe, but in Southeast Asia, Africa and the Americas as well. Why, then, were they not in general use throughout Oceania?

One explanation, that has been applied to other implements of various kinds in Micronesia and Polynesia, is the lack of proper materials. Good hunting and war bows require proper strong, springy wood. Wood meeting these specifications is scarce in the Pacific; on atolls and barren islands, wood of any kind is often entirely missing or is soft and fibrous. Too, the most powerful ancient bows were reinforced with horn. Oceania had no horned animals; nor did it have metal or strong animal gut for powerful strings.

However, it is apparent that the Menehune and the Chokalai had a tradition regarding the manufacture and use of a bow and applied this information when the materials were available. Both Ponape and Hawaii, with large forest growths, could supply better selections of wood. The black weapon-makers, possibly, turned to the sea to supply guts for strings. But the question still remains unsolved: Where did the black dwarfs get the knowledge and skill to make them?

On Ponape itself, the Micronesians who later inhabited the island, were extremely warlike. They used slings and war clubs, but also bows *taller than a man*. The arrows were tipped with a section of poisonous spine of the stingray. It is not unlikely that these late invaders inherited the use of bow and arrow from the Chokalai still living on the island.

Another extremely important weapon was the spear or lance. Spears were common throughout all of Micronesia and Polynesia. What made the Ponapean's bone-tipped spears important? They were sometimes twelve feet long! Other spears in Oceania were only half that length.

The Ponapeans used shell war horns. This was not common in Micronesia, although shell trumpets were used in Polynesia. A large conch shell, with a single note, served as a war trumpet. This type of conch trumpet was known in India and also in Crete.

Crete? The Greeks again. Was not Crete the home of Nearchus, the admiral of the Greek fleet, who sailed with Alexander when he invaded India?

Earlier, we noted that the Ponapeans used slings. It is reported that they were especially proficient with them. They also used war clubs. Both are extremely ancient weapons. Sling stones have been found in Iran (Persia) dating back to 1500 B.C. The Ponapean war club, however, was not of metal, but carved from heavy wood, and often inlaid with stones.

In contrast, the Polynesians did not use bows; their spears were short and with pointed heads of human bone. They favored war clubs and slings.

Although my interest centers on Micronesia, and Ponape in particular, there is good reason to investigate the Polynesians, too. If, as many ethnologists and anthropologists believe, the Polynesians were the last of the great migrations into Oceania and spreading to the eastern Pacific, and if part of this stream of migration made its way through Micronesia, then we might expect to find some social and cultural similarities between the two areas.

And I am still looking for an explanation of Nan Madol.

chapter
13

Of the Melanesians, Micronesians and Polynesians we have learned that the Melanesians were poor seafarers; the Micronesians were good, but not extraordinary; the Polynesians were not only excellent, but possibly the most able and adventuresome seamen of all time.

The Polynesians built fine, seaworthy craft. If trees were large enough, they hewed out the solid trunks with stone tools, shell chisels and adzes; sometimes they used controlled fires to burn out the required space. Some of the canoes were 70 feet long, 6 feet broad, and 4 feet deep. If large enough trees were not available, they then used smaller pieces "sewed" together. Separate pieces of wood were fastened by butting them closely, then sewing them together with roots and vegetable fibers. They did not use pegs. Seams were covered with skins and made watertight with resins and gums.

When completed, two canoes were doubled together; the parallel hulls were connected by planks between the two to form a deck or platform. Huts were erected on the platforms, and basketfuls of earth and sand were used to contain cooking fires.

Sails were made of matting. The masts were not permanent. Usually the sail was spread between two short masts, and under these conditions the pontoon-canoe could sail only before the wind. It had no rudder, but used a large steering paddle. They also added separate, high, carved bow and stern pieces similar to the old Greek galleys.

Some of the double canoes, however, had lateen sails and these could sail into the wind. Early reports by European explorers expressed amazement at these native craft that could out-perform their own ships. Estimates have placed the range of these Polynesian boats at 2,500 miles and, with a favorable wind, they probably reached a speed of seven knots.

In wonderment at the Polynesian craft, it is sometimes easy to forget that the Micronesians, especially in the Carolines, also built excellent canoes. They, too, built double outriggers and there is evidence to indicate they had an idea of a true quarter rudder. Symbolic bow figures were not lacking on their craft, either. Some of the figures resembled the lotus figureheads from Egypt.

Polynesians not only were skilled in boat building, but were equally accomplished in the science and art of navigation. Many readers are already familiar with the primitive "stick charts" sold in tourist shops in the South Pacific. These are fronds tied together to form a frame. Other fronds are laced into position up and down, across and diagonally on it. Small shells are tied in position to designate various islands and atolls. Leaf strips indicated reefs and treacherous seas. For the limited areas these "charts" were intended to cover, the information was remarkably accurate. On extended voyages, a series of such charts was carried by the old Polynesian voyagers.

Two hundred different names were assigned to identifiable stars by the Polynesians. On long voyages, at night they steered by the stars; by the sun during the day. The navigators knew in what part of the heavens the stars would appear, and in any month, when they were above the horizon. The ancient Hawaiians knew the planets Mercury, Venus, Mars, Jupiter and Saturn.

They also identified the solstice. The Polynesians divided

The Polynesian catamarans were among the most seaworthy of all ocean sailing craft. Some were eighty feet long and carried from one hundred to two hundred passengers as well as provisions. If the ship was on a colonizing expedition it also carried livestock—together with plantings and seedlings for the new homes. There is no evidence that the Micronesians developed such ships, but it is the author's theory that the catamaran was a logical development from the outrigger.

Outrigger sailing canoes were built by Micronesians and used in Ponape and throughout the Carolines. This type of craft was not a catamaran. The Micronesians also built large outrigger canoes that were propelled by paddles; they survive today only for ceremonial purposes.

the year into seasons, months and days. They counted 30 days to a month and intercalculated five days, about December 20, to make a year of 365 days.

This might indicate why, and how, the early Polynesians, coming up through Micronesia, could head *east* with some assurance of reaching the far-flung eastern islands in the Pacific.

Consider the distances, for instance, from the Carolines to Hawaii. Roughly, between feasible landing places, they are 400, 300, 210, 60, 70, 50, 80, 120, 130, 240, 110 and 1,900 miles. And this in an expanse of water stretching to the sky-ocean horizon in all directions. We can begin to understand how many of these ancient voyagers, thousands, perhaps tens of thousands, could easily be lost in time, distance and storms.

Dr. Kenneth P. Emory, distinguished authority of the Bishop Museum in Honolulu, wrote, concerning "The Coming of the Polynesians," for the *National Geographic*, in 1974:

> These ancients were remarkable seamen and no less skillful boat builders to have shaped craft capable of such voyages. . . . Its design favored the survival of persons with stamina, muscle, and ample fat to insulate the body from the deadly chill of wind evaporation upon spray-drenched skin. Rigorous selective pressures, oft repeated, may explain the physique and large size that distinguish Polynesians from other equatorial peoples.

This possibly is a case, as is pointed out, where the seagoing canoe may have helped "shape" the people.

The great Polynesian seagoing craft carried a navigator—a highly honored and respected man, second only to the king or chief, commanding the company and crew. Dr. David Lewis, writing in the same issue of the *National Geographic* quoted above, describes his experience with such a navigator, an aged, but still active Polynesian named Trevake. In his ketch, Dr. Lewis was making a long sea trip without maps and navigational aids except for the expert knowledge of old Trevake.

They set out before dawn, but before the stars had faded,

heavy clouds shut down their visibility. Soon they were hampered by rain squalls. The wind veered constantly.

Dr. Lewis writes,

> Yet, for eight solid hours, with never a moment's respite, Trevake stood with his feet planted wide apart on the foredeck. He held a *lo lop* palm leaf as an umbrella, his sopping wet lavalava flapping around his legs, concentrating intently on the sea, unmindful of chill and weariness, his only movement an occasional gesture to the helmsman.
>
> He held course by keeping a particular swell from the east-northeast, unfelt by me, dead astern.
>
> "It is *hao hua dele tai,* the sea wave," he (Trevake) said. "It lift up stern without rolling boat. Must wait for it long time, maybe ten minute. It not there all time."

Dr. Lewis explains that it may seem incredible that a man could find his way across the open Pacific by means of a slight swell that probably had its origin thousands of miles away, in the northeast trades beyond the Equator.

Old Trevake made a perfect landfall.

Another time, when visiting in Tonga, Lewis relates, he gleaned additional navigational advice from a native skipper named Kaloni Kienga on how to avoid reefs in that reef-strewn archipelago. Kienga pointed to a star in the constellation of Leo and told Lewis that when it (the star) had moved too high and far to the left, he was to follow the next star to rise from the same point on the horizon. Then the next, and so on until dawn. According to Kienga, this was the *kaveinga,* or the star path.

The vast Pacific, according to the old navigators, was divided into "seas." Each sea had a particular type of current which was recognizable by its "feel" even on the darkest nights. They also took advantage of the *te lapa.* These are streaks and flashes of light appearing well below the water's surface and they dart out from directions in which the islands lie, but disappear within sight of land. *Te lapa* are quite different from the usual, quite common, surface luminescence.

Thus, using solely their sea sense, and knowledge of natural phenomena, the early Polynesians ranged over an area greater than all the Soviet Union and China combined.

To quote Dr. Emory again:

> Had the first Polynesian settlers encountered an earlier people on the islands, one would expect that some vestige of an unrelated tongue would have survived. Linguistic researchers have detected none. They have found, however, that the languages of Polynesia have a common origin with those in Melanesia, Micronesia and Indonesia. All of them belong to one great Austronesian family that extends as far westward as Madagascar.

This brings up another possible clue for us to consider. It may or may not be important, and at this time it is impossible to prove a connection between some few existing place-names.

Dr. Mario Pei, eminent linguist, wrote in his book *The Story of Language:*

> If there are some fifty recognized sounds in a language like English, a more or less equal number in French, German, Spanish, Italian, and Russian, and these sounds seldom exactly coincide, then what is the total number of possible speech-sounds in all the existing tongues? No one has ever counted them, but, as may be surmised, they run into thousands.

From this we may deduce that it should not be an unexpected coincidence to discover a few identical-sounding words in both of two entirely different tongues. The law of probability would indicate that among thousands of possible "sounds" some duplications might occur, although their meanings differed.

Dr. Pei also points out that historical linguists usually make much of place-names. Even when a territory changes hands, the place-names normally remain. In addition, he wrote, names "are often bestowed upon lands not by their own inhabitants, but by neighbors."

This brings us to a remarkable "coincidence":

Candia is a very old name for the island of Crete in the Mediterranean.

Kandia is a mountainous tract in India.

Kandy in central Ceylon is famous for Buddhist temples. This is in the Indian Ocean off the southern tip of India.

Three very old place-names, almost identical, but separated by a distance of half a world. This could be a coincidence; it can also not be a coincidence. Toponymy, the study of place-names, is a science in itself. If these words are more than merely an example of curios—freak examples of similar sounds—then I am running into my old friends the Greeks again.

Perhaps it is time to take a look at Mediterranean sailing and compare it with the ships and seamanship to be found in Oceania. What, if anything, did the two groups have in common? And, equally important, where did they differ?

By the time the Greeks became a sea power, they had inherited much knowledge from the Egyptians and the Phoenicians, who were the best sailors of the Old World. Marine and river transportation were known from very early times in Egypt—as far back as 4000 B.C. These craft undoubtedly had sails. By 3000 B.C., Egyptian boats were sailing the eastern Mediterranean. In Europe, water transportation is at least as old as the Mesolithic, about 5000 B.C.

The Phoenicians quickly learned to adapt from others. Their first ships were hardly more than large canoes, but they soon discovered that rowers facing aft were more efficient than paddling. They developed two types of ships: one was the war galley, which was long and narrow, with many oars and a small square sail; the other was a merchantman, short and tubby, with few oars and a large square sail.

Oarsmen were not slaves, but well-paid free workers. Slave rowers came much later. The Phoenicians developed a deck over the rowers; above the deck the war galleys carried armed soldiers. Later the galleys carried rams in the bows, and the bows and the oars became multitiered. Eventually, these large ships carried hundreds of men including the crew and soldiers.

In the early days of sailing, cautious Mediterranean traders

The old Phoenicians were long considered the ancient world's greatest sailors. In ships like this 700 B.C. model they pushed into unknown waters—mostly for trading and commercial purposes. The Greeks, like most Mediterranean peoples, learned sailing and seamanship from the Phoenicians. In ships quite similar to this, manned by oars and a square sail, steered with double oars instead of a rudder, and with a high carved bow and stern, the Greeks made their way to India.

were seldom out of sight of land—the coast line. Only on occasions when they knew their exact locations did they sail across the Mediterranean with a backing breeze. A following wind was important in those early days when a loose billowing square sail was not capable of much manipulation. They were quickly torn to shreds in a really strong wind. In bad weather, or against the wind, the men took to their oars.

This does not mean that the ships "hugged the shore." Early on, the sailors learned to dread being driven on to a lee shore. Usually they stood out to sea to avoid dangers of hidden rocks, sandbanks, riptides and breakers, which are common threats of inshore waters. Too, there is evidence of early open-sea and cross-sea voyages in the Mediterranean, even before the days of sail. This would indicate that early pilots could steer by the sun in the day, and by the stars at night.

By the time the first sails were in common use, the pilots were, no doubt, familiar with the characteristics and behavior of winds from the different quarters. In addition, landmarks and coastal profiles as they appeared from the sea were stored in their memories. Wind meant the same as *direction,* so a seaman had to know to what country it would carry him.

125

The Greek navigators had many ingenious, although primitive, methods of navigation. A pilot could measure star altitude against the mast and rigging; the span of his wrist gave him an approximate altitude of 8 degrees, an outstretched hand was equivalent to 18 degrees. The knowledge of altitude gave him an idea whether he was north or south of his home port. These were probably the "clock stars" known in Egypt since 2500 B.C. It was easier for him to make latitude by staying on it and then searching east and west for longitude.

The Greek ships, incidentally, had rather deep keels. Their fighting ships were not built to carry water and provisions in quantity and could not spend more than a few days at sea without provisioning. Landmarks visible at a distance were always of utmost importance.

Did the Greeks use marine charts or maps? The answer: probably. They used maps freely for land travel and military expeditions. From the days of Darius the Great, a Persian king (558–486 B.C.), sailors had a *periplous*—a sort of compendium that gave distances between most of the important ports of the ancient world. For instance, "Coasting from the Pillars of Hercules (Gibraltar) to Cape Hermaea is two days." Distances were measured in a "day's sail." A day's sail was not meant as the actual time taken, but indicated a theoretical distance—which might vary between 40 and 60 miles.

Herodotus, in the fifth century B.C., specifically mentions a route map through Asia Minor. It is not improbable that sailors too had charts. If so, however, no one can estimate how detailed they were. It is unlikely, though, that the charts contained any parallels or meridians. Directions, probably, were indicated by prevailing winds.

Such terms as a "day's sail" or a "day's journey" are ambiguous. The word "day" may have two meanings: it can mean twenty-four hours when used in a calendar sense, or simply the time between sunrise and sunset. Chaucer, 1,700 years later, tells us that a peasant's day is reckoned "from dawn to dusk." Furthermore, we know that many of the old ships tied up at night, although others did not. Rounding capes, islands, deltas and reefs is not easy to measure.

So, at best, the theoretical distance of 40–60 miles is an approximation.

It is unfortunate that no Greek chart or map has managed to survive the more than two millennia since it was drawn.

Two devices the early seamen used were a sounding line and "shore-sighting" birds. An Egyptian tomb painting, about 1500 B.C., shows a long "sounding rod." From as early as the fifth century B.C., we know that sailors set a bird free when out of sight of land. If the bird caught sight of land on the distant horizon, it would wing in that direction, otherwise, it would return to the ship. A "land-sighting" bird served well for distances of 100–150 miles; beyond that they were not of much service.

In addition, the ancient mariners often were guided by migrating birds. A large flock followed by one long skein after another, sometimes covered a period of weeks. A course might be followed by watching the successive flights of birds passing overhead.

From earliest days, astronomy was closely tied to astrology. Evidence points to the Egyptians making astronomical observations possibly as early as 4000 B.C. The Babylonians too were very early astronomers, and from them the ancient Greeks learned to make their own observations. They took over the Babylonian findings and added their own interpretations. There is little doubt that the Greeks could and did use the stars and heavens to navigate when necessary. We know, of course, that the navigational stars change from the north to the south latitudes. If the old Greeks did not know the southern constellations, certainly many of the sailors they came in contact with, from other parts of the world, did know.

Perhaps now is as good a time as I will find to again bring up the subject of the compass. There appears to be little or no evidence that the compass came from China originally. A "south-pointing" chariot known from very ancient times in China is thought to be no magnetic instrument, but a mechanical toy. (Author's Note: I do not know what this proof is.) Around 1100 A.D., its use on shipboard is remarked upon in Chinese annals, but neither the Polynesians nor the Greeks, in their early voyages, had the use of one.

What they did have is well summed up in a description of the "Pilot" written in Sanskrit in 434 A.D.

> He [the skilled seaman] knows the course of the stars and can always orient himself; he knows the value of signs—both regular, accidental and abnormal, and of good and bad weather. He distinguishes the regions of the ocean by the fish, the colour of the water, the nature of the bottom, the birds, the mountains, and other indications.

Although this description was written seven hundred years after the time of the Greeks and their invasion of India, the words are still true concerning the earlier seamen.

It is interesting that the "Pilot" mentions the color of the water and the nature of the bottom (of the sea). Reports have it that the mouth of the Indus often swarmed with water-snakes (could they have been eels?) and was distinguished by very bright-blue-green water.

Ptolemy, the Greek Alexandrian geographer and mathematician, second century A.D., made a list of latitudes and longitudes covering the world as he knew it. The list was lost to history and was not recovered until the fifteenth century. Unfortunately, when the list was first lost, it was nearly five hundred years after our Greeks might have needed it, and obviously it was too late to do them any good at any time.

And finally, a word about mystic symbols. Some sea symbols are almost universal—the spiral, the fish, the Sea-Fan, and the anchor. Such symbols, of universal meaning, have a way of persisting through centuries and civilizations.

One such symbol, although not of the sea, was found in the great sea battle at Lepanto in 1571. The Turks recognized a standard with a two-headed eagle flying over the galley of Don John of Austria, their foe. The Turks too had once used this emblem! The two-headed eagle was an old Sumerian emblem originally found on the banks of the Euphrates. It had taken three or four thousand years to cross the length of the Mediterranean Sea from one end to the other. Once, too, it had been associated with the ancient Babylonian god Gilgamesh. The double-headed eagle continued in Russia down to the fall of the Tsars in this century.

However, none of the sea symbols mentioned above, or any other recognized symbol of any kind, has ever been found in Nan Madol.

chapter

14

Often I have ranged far afield looking for clues to the people who built this strange city on the tip of an isolated island deep in the Pacific. Sometimes I have gone so far back as the old Egyptians, the Sumerians, the Phoenicians, the Harappans, the Chinese, and the Classical and pre-Classical Greeks—not because I believe that Nan Madol actually was built by these old builders, but because the know-how of these men of ancient history might somehow have been passed on to, or acquired by, the men who did build it.

William Churchill, American ethnologist, 1912, wrote in his book *The Rapanui Speech and the Peopling of South East Polynesia* that the Cyclopean stone works are "utterly beyond our comprehension, since apparently [they are] so utterly beyond the present capacity of the islanders."

Many experts agree completely with Churchill.

Others, however, do not agree. They believe that some sudden, unexpected drive inspired the primitive aboriginal inhabitants to engineering feats that they have never been able to achieve again. It is difficult to accept, though, that a comparatively small population, with no experience and little *interest* in stone working, could have—quite out of the blue—quarried the huge stones, transported them, and then erected the gigantic stone city. One is almost inclined to side with the old Ponapean legend that the stones flew through the air by magic.

One point that I have discovered in this investigation may perhaps be puzzling you, too. Not even small portable stone images have been observed in Micronesia or in central or western Polynesia. Not until farthest east, on the Marquesas and Easter Island, are they found. On Easter Island, of course, are the tremendous stone heads that have made the island famous.

Carving stone images or statues is a creative art. On Ponape the huge stone buildings required engineering and design, but not creative ability like that of a painter or sculptor. Basalt, such as is found on Ponape, is very hard and it is difficult to work into good carvings. On Easter Island the stone, a volcanic tuff, was excellent for the purpose.

According to their legends, the Easter Islanders arrived in two canoes under their Polynesian chief, Hotu Matu, about eight hundred years ago. They were very warlike and were cannibals. They brought with them a system of writing on boards, *rongo-rongo,* and a religion that demanded, in some way, the raising of the huge statues. Consequently, the sculpting and raising of the huge stone heads were not only a creative project, but a religious one as well. The nearest neighbors to the Easter Islanders are the Marquesans, 2,300 miles to the northwest.

The subject of rongo-rongo writing has long been a matter of speculation among experts. Some say that it is not writing, that at best it is pictographs that the islanders could not read and was used as "memory joggers" to help them recite oral material.

Easter Island lore asserts that the first king brought 67 tablets with him. These tablets (rongo-rongo) contained allegories, traditions, genealogical tables, and proverbs. Knowledge of these strange characters was confined to the family, the chiefs of the six districts on the island, the sons of chiefs, and certain priests or teachers. The people could not, or were not permitted to, read them. Once a year the tablets were read aloud to all the assembled people.

To this day, the tablets are undeciphered.

In 1932, Guillaume de Hevesy tried to establish a connection between the scripts of the Indus Valley seals and the Easter Island rongo-rongo. His efforts caused quite a commotion.

Alfred Métraux, ethnologist, in his book *The Proto-Indian Scripts and the Easter Island Tablets* in 1938, wrote: "No unbiased man who studies the tablets and the Indus script can fail to notice the enormous difference not only in the system, but in the form and type of the signs."

Other specialists upheld Métraux, quoting the fantastic spaces of land, water and time that separate the Easter Island tablets from any contact with the Indus Valley seals. They also point out that the boustrophedon arrangement of lines (with each alternate line upside down) was unknown in the Indus Valley. In addition, they argue that Mohenjo Daro (and Harappa) is dated around 2000 B.C., and the symbols could not have survived a journey of 13,000 miles of ocean and islands, leaving no trace en route over a span of some 3,000 years.

But, apparently, they did survive in one way or another. Look at the comparison of the "characters" between the two systems of writing. If it is sheer coincidence, then it is unbelievable!

Other authorities of distinction believe that rongo-rongo boards are of comparatively recent date and point to the fact that some of the boards (there is no wood on Easter Island) come from the ash blades of Western oars used in small boats of eighteenth-century sailing ships. This indicates, to me, the possibility that these boards may have been *copied* on oar blades from the visiting sailing ships, but, it does not necessarily prove when or where the writing, originally, was created. Other tablets were copied on boards salvaged from driftwood.

The Indus Valley seals have been found far distant, from their homeland, in Mesopotamia. This established contact between the two civilizations nearly four thousand years ago.

A comparison of three "scripts" (very similar in appearance) from three civilizations vastly separated by time and distance. At left is writing from the Indus Valley in India, circa 2500–1700 B.C. At center, the rongo-rongo script of Easter Island. At right, writing from Crete and Greece from 2000–1550 B.C. (COURTESY OF *True* MAGAZINE)

But, like Easter Island rongo-rongo, the Indus Valley script cannot be read today, either. It puzzles me how the systems can be compared.

Let me advance a possibility. At this point, it is not a theory, but it is certainly worth considering. Could the memories of picture writing have been carried by Indus sailors long after their civilization was destroyed? Although the system was forgotten, the symbols remained. Very early, a particular Polynesian royal family might have carried written heirlooms along, recopying the old wooden tablets when necessary to ensure their continuation. Eventually, even this meaning was lost, and only a memory of what the tablets contained remained in an oral version.

The Easter Island legends referred to earlier concerning King Hotu Matu and his 67 tablets state that he brought them with him from the island of Marae-renga. But other cultural and mythical evidence points to the Marquesas and possibly to Mangareva, as lands of origin of the Easter Island people. Yet these lands (or islands) have no memory of such tablets. This prompts the question: Did the rongo-rongo tablets come from a land beyond Polynesia?

No, some experts say. They do not believe rongo-rongo to be a true script. Possibly, they agree, they served as memory joggers. The many different signs were developed to avoid monotony and repetition of the few main motifs derived from the island's bird cult.

In *Die Osterinselschrift,* written by R. von Heine-Geldern, in 1938, the author states that in his opinion the Easter Island writing was imported from the Indus Valley.

Although most experts define the "characters" of Indus writing as pictographic, Thor Heyerdahl claims that rongo-rongo is hieroglyphic. There is a difference, although both are methods of picture writing. Pictographs, simply, are pictures that represent ideas. Hieroglyphics (we think of the ancient Egyptians) are highly conventionalized symbols to represent ideas. Another, not so well known definition of hieroglyphics, is "a figure or symbol with a hidden meaning."

Heyerdahl has an interesting tale concerning rongo-rongo. He says that it is mentioned in the most ancient legends and that on certain islands, "Rongo" is pronounced *Lo-no*. Lono is the name of one of the Polynesians' best-known legendary ancestors, and he is expressly described as white-skinned with fair hair. This legend was related to Heyerdahl by a very old man on the island of Raroia. The old man went on to add that in truly ancient times, rongo-rongo was also used to name really large *pae-paes*, or rafts, but it was no longer used. Only about twenty specimens of rongo-rongo tablets remain and they are in museums around the world.

Alfred Métraux maintains that some things about rongo-rongo are fairly clear. The tablets were extremely sacred objects surrounded by taboos. Very early, the tablets' users intoned chants in front of the boards without trying to spell out the individual characters. Supposedly, signs were arbitrarily associated with chants, each symbol representing a significant word, a phrase, a sentence or even a verse. Gradually, and quite naturally, the symbols' significance deteriorated until they were completely forgotten.

However, tradition tells us that the tablets were brought to Easter Island. Whatever they were, they were developed *before* arrival. It may also be pointed out that similarities in the pictographic signs of different cultures are to be expected, since the sign of a fish or a bird or other common image will

The famous old story-boards of the island of Palau were crude, but the "figures" were not unlike the "symbols" found in rongo-rongo writing on Easter Island—thousands of miles to the east, just off the coast of South America. Some authorities believe that long ago a connection between the two systems of communication did occur, regardless of the distance. The people of Palau are Micronesian; the Eastern Islanders are Polynesian. (COURTESY OF CONTINENTAL AIRLINES/AIR MICRONESIA)

look the same in any language. A pictographic system can hardly be called *writing* in a true sense.

From time to time there have been vague reports that samples of rongo-rongo have popped up in the Carolines. I have been unable to track such reports down to an authoritative source. However, an interesting situation does exist on the island of Palau.

Palau is located in the Carolines, roughly 1,200 miles west of Ponape, and is recognized for its "story boards." These story boards are carved wooden panels, colored with natural dyes, and are a Palauan institution. The themes are often sexual. Today they are sold to tourists; each story board is accompanied by a synopsis in English of the story it tells.

Actually, a story board and a rongo-rongo tablet are definitely different. Both are painted and/or carved on wood; and each tells "something" to some degree. Originally, story boards were quite large and often were carved on the front of houses.

135

Are they even distantly related? Who knows? But the two systems are pictograph representations of written ideas. It is not impossible that they both began with some common point of reference—and then went their different ways. Too, if rongo-rongo ever appeared in the Carolines, it might have been mistaken for the story boards; and vice versa, the unexpected appearance of a story board might give rise to the reported sightings of rongo-rongo.

The known signs of the Indus Valley script number slightly fewer than four hundred, about half the number in the earlier Sumerian pictographic script. This is still far too many signs for an alphabet, so experts believe the script must have been basically syllabic. It seems to have been written from right to left, then back again in the boustrophedon manner. No cursive writing was ever developed; even signs scratched on potsherds are in the exact pictographic form.

The entire collection of Indus inscriptions from seals, pottery, and copper amulets shows no development. The signs appear fully formed, accents and all, and do not change. This rigidity appears typical of the Indus Valley civilization. The society and its culture remained without change from beginning to end except for *one new* pot form.

The old Egyptian civilization was notorious for its conservatism. It would appear that the Indus Valley was even more so; it seems to have ossified.

In *The Past,* edited by Leonard Cottrell, a reference to the Indus Valley writing says: "The script, which bears no resemblance to any other, seems to have been an arbitrary product, the result of a knowledge of writing rather than an evolved one." If it were taken over, already developed to a certain point and never further advanced, then from whom did the Harappans take it? Also, might not the Polynesians of Easter Island have done the same?

Again, do not forget that neither the Indus Valley script nor Easter Island rongo-rongo can be deciphered, or read. Comparison is impossible.

Perhaps eventually these systems of writing will be read. The more examples the experts can work from, the better their chances of success. It is not probable that many more examples of rongo-rongo will ever be discovered. Further archaeological digging at Indus Valley sites may unearth more examples from that civilization.

Writing, in all civilizations, was done on the surface of some local material. The Egyptians used paper made of strips of papyrus reed. The Mesopotamians wrote on slabs of clay. In India, paper was made from palm fronds; the Chinese used strips of bamboo. Stone, wood, and leather have also been utilized. Early writings on stone and clay bricks have survived. The other materials, being perishable, have almost completely disappeared.

Indus and Easter Island writing bears no resemblance to Chinese, yet the "idea" behind them may be similar. Chinese writing began as a series of pictures—one word per picture. However, it never evolved into a phonetic alphabet, although it became conventionalized and compounded to make up Chinese characters. The characters have remained as logographs (word-signs) or ideographs (idea-signs) with a different sign being needed for each word.

In 1908, the Thilenius South Seas Expedition recorded a mysterious and quite unexplainable counting system on Faraulep. Faraulep is a small atoll situated about 850 miles west and slightly north of Ponape in the Yap district of the Carolines. The Faraulep islanders had a regular, stepped, series of "characters" representing numbers ranging in amounts from 100,000 to 60,000,000! The characters resemble no other figures or numerals used anywhere. (See illustration, page 139.) Furthermore, the extremely high numbers have no apparent use in the daily life of a people living on a very small, sandy atoll. *What* could they possibly use them for? Six million is an incomprehensible amount or figure to an educated sophisticated man. Some authorities believe the numbers might have been carried over by the islanders from their previous culture, before they migrated to the more distant islands.

The use of numbers leads me to a system of knotted cords, similar to the well-known Inca *quipu*, that is found in Micronesia and Polynesia. This system is especially useful in remembering numbers and it can also be used, to some extent, to keep records—especially genealogies. This does not necessarily imply a connection between the Incas and the far-western Pacific.

"Lost languages" are not unusual. Even with the use of advanced modern techniques, some have remained unsolved. The Phaistos Disc, found in Crete in 1908, is a good example. The Disc, dated to 1700 B.C., is pictographic, inscribed in spirals and subdivided by vertical lines into sections. It contains 241 signs with 45 different characters, and it is probable that the writing progressed from right to left, beginning at the outside of the Disc and continuing to the inside, ending at the center. The 45 signs it contains do not constitute the entire system. Experts believe perhaps it had 60 signs, with individual words consisting of two to five signs. The writing is syllabic and of the Aegean type. (Author's Note: To me there is in the signs some similarity to those of rongo-rongo. See illustration, page 133.)

Sir Arthur Evans discovered hieroglyphic tablets in Crete; he called them Linear A, and they date from between 1750 and 1450 B.C. These read from left to right, and have never been deciphered either. Linear A was replaced by Linear B, the exact date unknown but sometime around 1400 B.C. Unquestionably B was derived from Linear A, which in turn can be traced back to hieroglyphic writing and possibly the Phaistos Disc. Linear B contained over a hundred word signs; its ideograms sometimes incorporate a syllabic sign. (Author's Note: Again, to me personally, there is some similarity to the Indus Valley writing. See illustration, page 133.)

Linear B was deciphered by Michael Ventris, who discovered the key in 1952. Unfortunately, Ventris was killed in an auto accident in 1956, before he could accomplish more of his brilliant work.

Jumping from Linear B, 1400 B.C., to eighth-century Greece, spans nearly seven hundred years. In Greece, in the eighth century B.C., each little state had its own dialect of spoken, as well as written, language. In 776 B.C., the Greeks adopted the Phoenician alphabet, from which all other present alphabets have descended.

In the search through linguistics, mother tongues are divided into separate languages. As noted earlier, in the Americas

100 000	200 000	300 000	400 000
500 000	600 000	700 000	800 000
900 000	1 000 000	2 000 000	3 000 000
4 000 000	5 000 000	6 000 000	7 000 000
8 000 000	9 000 000	10 000 000	20 000 000
30 000 000	40 000 000	50 000 000	60 000 000

These symbols are part of a counting system that was recorded by members of the Thilenius South Seas Expedition on Faraulep in 1908. Symbols for such extremely high numbers have no apparent use in the daily life of a small atoll; they might be remains of the people's previous culture before their migration to the outer islands.
(COURTESY OF THE UNITED STATES TRUST TERRITORY DEPARTMENT OF EDUCATION)

more than three hundred separate and distinct linguistic stocks existed. Too, in Micronesia, neighboring tribes are often unintelligible to one another, even some that are dwelling side by side. Consider this question: How long would it take for such neighboring tribes to develop languages that were mutually unintelligible and completely different in structure?

The answer: Certainly a *very* long time.

It is a definite handicap that nothing is known about the Indus Valley language. As we know, Hevesy attempted to find an answer connecting Harappan and rongo-rongo. The late Professor Stephen H. Langdon, Assyriologist, confirmed that the similarity of the Indus Valley writing and rongo-rongo is truly remarkable.

A language may be spoken, yet never develop to a stage of writing. From one end to the other of the vast east-west Caroline archipelago is almost as far as from New York City to Venezuela in South America. So it is not surprising, perhaps, to find so many tongues spoken, as well as different cultures and divided societies within the Carolines.

What did the builders of Nan Madol speak?

I do not know.

chapter

15

Every so often we come across a tantalizing bit of information. In the last chapter, it was stated that 4,000-year-old
Indus Valley seals have been found in far-off Mesopotamia.
This leads us to another. In Polynesia is found the name "Uru"
(also "Ulu" in dialects). It is remembered as the name of a
principal people living in or bordering on the central original
homeland of the Polynesians. In his *Origin of the Maori*
(1923), Elsdon Best shows the necessity of going back to far
Asia Minor to find an analogy. He quotes (from the Maori
Record Articles [1905–06]): "In the southern part of Sumeria,
near the mouth of the Euphrates river, as then situated,
existed about 2800 B.C. the flourishing state of Uru, known
as Ur of the Chaldees to the readers of the Scriptures." Best
also speculates that *Irihia*, in the Maori, is a reference to
India. The *nd* sound is alien to the Maori tongue and was
changed to *rih.*

In most investigative cases, one clue leads to another. But
not always. A bright trail may string out and grow dim, eventually to fade completely. On more than one occasion I have
followed the Polynesians, although my main concern is with

the Micronesians. I have done this because the Polynesians were before them. It is probable that one of the Polynesian routes was through Micronesia. If it was, then possibly they might have made contact with the Ponapeans and—someway, somehow—carried the evidence with them. I have searched for proof of Old World and Asian influence in Oceania that would help explain the riddle of Nan Madol. This far along, I seem to find as many clues, indirect ones, among the Polynesians as among the Micronesians. And these clues continue to point to the Greeks.

The earliest civilizations all seemed to be organized in much the same way: the king, royal family and relatives, the priesthood, possibly an assembly of the richest and most powerful men, and the warriors. Women, poor men and slaves did not count. This would serve to describe most of the old civilizations—including what we know about Nan Madol.

According to Ashley Montagu, every nonliterate society has medicine men, priests, elders of the council, skilled artists, skilled stoneworkers, skilled woodworkers, metalworkers, educators, engineers, food providers, soldiers, et cetera. He also points out that religion is the main bond that binds humans together—the bond of relatedness. No people of whom we have knowledge is without a religion.

Émile Durkheim (1858–1917), a French sociologist, regarded religion as the most primitive of all social phenomena.

When applying these criteria to Nan Madol, I find some important elements present, but also many are missing. It is true that Nan Madol probably represented a nonliterate society. It is not known whether "medicine men" were linked with the priesthood, but apparently the society had no skilled artists, no skilled stoneworkers, in the sense of sculptors, although it might have had, and probably did possess, skilled woodworkers. No trace of metalworkers has been found. Food providers—fishermen and farmers—it certainly had. Soldiers and warriors, too. Nan Madol itself proves the existence of engineers. It practiced a religion based on a turtle cult, of which little is known. What is known, is this:

After death, the body was oiled and perfumed, and rolled in a mat with a few personal belongings. The body was taken from islet to islet within the city, accompanied by traditional dancing and ceremonial *saku* drinking. It was then buried on one of the many islets—depending on the importance of the deceased. The body remained buried, but after three nights, the soul (Ngehn) left the body to descend to a heavenly place beneath the ocean called *Pahsed*. After another short stay in *Pahsed*, the soul ascended to *Lahng Apap*, a lower heaven in which a treacherous spinning bridge was located. The bridge, *Kehnkepir*, spanned a large, black pit—*Pwelko*. Successfully crossing the bridge, *Kehnkepir*, a soul was free to wander and live in all three spheres, or *Lahngs*: first heaven, the home of god; the second, home of spirits; and the third, below the ocean. To fall off the bridge, while crossing it, plunged the soul into the black pit for eternity. Before crossing, a soul prepared itself by singing a song (perhaps a ceremonial chant or incantation). If sung well enough, a successful crossing was ensured!

If nothing else, the ancient Ponapeans held a belief in an afterlife, complete with heavens and hell.

The Greeks were an aristocratic society based on slavery. Authentic Greek history begins around 700 B.C. Between 500 and 400 B.C., the century has been called the "Golden Age." The Greeks were interested in ideas and did not hesitate to borrow them from the Egyptians, Babylonians and the Phoenicians. As a people, the Greeks seem to have been more interested in the humanities, but became extremely practical when it was necessary.

Long preceding the Greek civilization, was the Minoan. Crete was a great sea power from 2400 to 1400 B.C. Its people built beautiful palaces, but around 1700 B.C., an unknown catastrophe devastated it badly. It rebuilt and continued for another 300 years or so, then began to fade. The Cretan culture might have held on, someway, until as late as 400 B.C. By this time, however, the island was denuded of forests, and the Cretans could no longer build their superb sea galleys, on which their maritime power depended.

Although the sea civilization of Crete collapsed, the island became a base for pirates who roved the Mediterranean for centuries. The Cretan sailors were fearless and aggressive.

Other Mediterranean states often hired them as mercenaries in their sea battles.

During and after the great days of Crete, Greek kings built their thick Cyclopean walls at Mycenae and Tiryns. These walls contained enormous stones with smaller stones plugging the gaps between the larger ones.

The ancient Greeks had long learned how to build sea walls and bastions against surging water for their own ports. They had learned this from the Phoenicians, who through necessity had built such walls to protect their ports along unindented coasts where they had established trading colonies.

Early Greek temples were boxlike stone structures with wooden roofs. Sometimes the center of the temple was left open to the sky, because the Greeks never invented a true roof truss—a series of beams joined together to form a rigid structure made up of triangles. Consequently, their engineers used posts and lintels. Later, they used stone architraves, horizontally resting on stone columns, to hold up the roof. They also substituted roof tiles for wooden shingles.

The Greeks did not use mortar. Instead, they carefully trimmed stones to an accurate fit, then bonded the stone blocks together with iron cramps. It was not until late Roman times that the Greeks used the arch.

Their houses followed the familiar pattern with blank walls facing the street, and all rooms opening on a central courtyard. Their towns and cities provided no drainage systems and no paved roads.

In many areas, the ancient Greek engineers were accomplished builders. They drained marshes, and in fifth-century Sicily, where they had established a colony, they provided an elaborate system of water channels and tanks to furnish the colonists with water from nearby sources. These old water mains are still there.

On the island of Samos they dug a 3,300-foot tunnel, 5½ feet wide and deep beneath a 900-foot-high hill. The floor contained a three-foot-deep trench to hold a large clay pipe to carry water. Digging on the tunnel started from both ends to meet at the center. A perfect join up was missed. The miss was by a considerable distance, so there was a kink in the middle of the tunnel. But for the builders to come even that close, they had to have used some kind of surveying instruments, although what kind is not known.

A Greek physicist, Straton, around 287 B.C., wrote a book entitled *Mechanics*. (This was thirty-six years after the death of Alexander.) In his book, Straton discusses the law of the lever and another device he calls "gear-wheels." We have no indication whether the "gear wheels" were in general use, or even what they were for. However, later, such wheels were used in small machines, in the temples, to sprinkle water. In addition to applying the law of the lever to the oars of galleys, the author also devotes space to counterweights, the roller, the wedge, the pulley, the sling, the capstan and windlass. These are all simple mechanical devices, but important ones, and how many were known and used earlier than Straton's writings, we do not know, but it is reasonable to assume that some, if not all, were in use earlier. Certainly, the devices were not all discovered at once and just in time for Straton to write about them. For instance, the wedge, roller and lever were used as far back as the ancient Egyptians. The Assyrians used pulleys to draw water from deep wells in the eighth century B.C.

In old warfare, an armed man on top of a wall had a decided advantage over his foe climbing up. The defender could shoot an arrow, cast a javelin, thrust with a spear, or drop crushing stones, scalding hot water or red-hot sand. He could also push away the scaling ladder with a forked pole.

But, preceding the time of Alexander, the Greeks had no siege machines or engines of war except, possibly, a battering ram, and they might have shot flaming arrows. Alexander, for the first time, used a stone-throwing catapult in his siege of Tyre in 332 B.C. Immediately, the Greek cities, to protect themselves against catapults, began to dig ditches and sometimes moats filled with water to keep the war machines at a distance. Is it possible that the canals of Nan Madol were for defensive purposes as well as simple marine transportation?

Earlier, when the canals of Nan Madol were discussed, we saw that only canoes or very small boats could successfully use them. They would not accommodate Greek galleys either. But it is interesting to read that Dionysios the Elder, Tyrant of Syracuse in 399 B.C., forty-three years before Alexander, started experimenting with larger ships containing *five* banks of oars—called *penteres*. Two or more men manned each oar. Some ships probably had four or five men to an oar. These *penteres* had a frame or an *outrigger*, an *apostis*, in which the oars pivoted. This early recognition of an outrigger might be important.

Alexander, too, was the first soldier known to have worn an iron helmet. In addition, he wore metal breast and back plates, greaves, et cetera. An ordinary soldier, of course, could not afford to buy such expensive equipment, nor could the army afford to supply them. In the time of the Persian King Darius I, around 490 B.C., the Greeks used a bronze helmet, leather body armor studded with bronze buttons, and bronze greaves to protect the legs. This was, probably, the armor still worn by the common foot soldiers in Alexander's army, and they used wooden shields covered with heavy leather.

But cavalrymen and sailors had to save weight. The cavalry preferred a corselet made of several layers of linen canvas glued together and molded on a form. The result was a hard, light, form-fitting armor similar to modern laminated plastic.

In Alexander's fleet, the sailors wore short tunics, covered with a quilted or leather armor. This protection was more flexible, permitting them to get around the ship quickly, and if they fell into the sea, the metal weight would not drown them immediately. The common crewman wore a fez of leather or heavy felt. The officers might have worn a Grecian helmet and armor, both for protection and as a symbol of rank.

The Polynesians wore helmets, tight-fitting caps of wickerwork, surmounted by a curved crest *exactly* the same shape as Greek helmets of Alexander's day. (See illustration, page 147.) Also, some Polynesians protected themselves with heavy bark corsets; others wore quilted armor or armor made of rods. Another type of armor that was popular had wooden breast and back plates; the sides were covered with a heavy bark cloth. It was bound on with ropes.

The Micronesians also used armor. A comparison of weap-

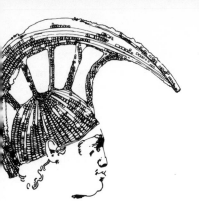

Notice the striking similarity between ancient Greek and Polynesian dress. The Grecian helmets (right) were made of metal and sported dyed horsehair plumes. The Polynesians had neither metal nor horses but constructed their helmets (left) from wickerwork and often covered them with the bright feathers of birds. These offered only slight protection and probably served as a status symbol. (COURTESY OF True MAGAZINE)

ons between the peoples of Oceania and the Mediterranean shows us something, too.

The Greeks used bows of two different types: one was made of a kind of antelope horn; the other was made of flexible wood. The bowstring was of plaited horsehair or ox gut. They had slings, war clubs, short stabbing swords, javelins to throw, and long, broad-bladed spears. Their shields, *peltas*, were either round, square, or crescent-shaped. The Greek foot soldiers' main offensive weapon was a stabbing spear; he used his short, broad, chopping sword only when his spear was lost or broken. The famous Greek phalanx, equipped with spears eighteen feet long, bristling rank upon rank, was almost impenetrable.

As I have pointed out, bows are few in Oceania, due, perhaps, to lack of proper materials. Slings were common because they were simple to make and small stones are found everywhere. So were warclubs. The Polynesians did have short, deadly wooden swords studded with shark teeth and sharp stones along the edges. Some authorities say that the Polynesian spears with broad blades of razor-sharp bamboo are wooden copies of metal forms. Bamboo, too, was used for daggers.

147

On the island of Ponape, a striking coincidence appears. The longest spears of any found in Oceania appeared in Ponape. Ponapean spears were often twelve feet in length! This is far longer than those used by other Micronesians or Polynesians, which are from five to seven feet. Is the tradition behind the Ponapean spear connected with the eighteen-foot spear used with such deadly effect by the Greek phalanxes of old?

Curiously enough, another similarity appears between the Greeks and the Oceanic peoples. The Greeks had spear-throwers made of throngs. A spear-thrower is a rather sophisticated idea. The Micronesians and Polynesians also had spear-throwers, but made of wood. By means of such a device, a thrown spear is given tremendous impetus by the added length of the spear-thrower. By such means a hunter or warrior increases the leverage of his arm. A seven-foot javelin may be thrown 60–70 yards from a man's hand. Using a spear-thrower, the distance can be increased to 150 yards.

On the island of Yap, in the far-western area of the Carolines, another puzzle has long existed—the presence of "money"! The islanders have, from very ancient times, established a unique form of wealth. Yapmen sail to the island of Palau, a round trip of over 800 miles, to mine a certain kind of rock. The rock is not precious in any way, but from it the Yapmen mine large blocks of stone. The rock is chipped off to resemble a round wheel, and a small hole is drilled or chipped in the center. Some of the "wheels" are extremely large and heavy—up to seven and eight feet high and weighing tons. Others are much smaller, some only a few inches in diameter. The Yap islanders consider them as money; they are called *fei*. The heavy, round, stone wheels are transported on rafts towed behind canoes back to Yap. The stone money is erected around the island and seldom moved again. Title to it is jealously guarded, even though it changes owners. A large stone wheel beside a village, may represent the villagers' entire wealth. Even today, in Yap, the *fei* is valued over inflationary currencies.

How and when this odd custom began is not known. So far as the Yapmen are concerned, "it has always been so." The stones themselves have no mineral value; they are not beautiful, and they have absolutely no artistic merit. At best, the stones are crude, rough stone, circular wheels put to no practical or religious use, and all they represent is many man-hours of toil.

In 1948, Philippe Diolé, of the French National Museums, led an underwater expedition at the old Mediterranean port of *Fos-sur-Mer.* "Fos" is a very ancient port that has been neglected by history, forgotten and lost. Diolé discovered anchors of ancient Greek ships buried in the mud of the sea bottom. It is evident that the old ships used three kinds of anchors. Some of the anchors were pyramid-shaped, of stone, pierced near the top or with juglike handles for attaching cables. Another type was wooden anchors, weighted and covered with lead sheathing. Much later, this type of anchor was made of iron.

Finally, a third kind of anchor was a rough, round, flat stone with a hole in the center to attach the cable! Shaped like a wheel, these anchors are almost an exact duplication of the Yap islanders' stone money!

From these facts, one might propose a theory. Yap Island is farthest west of all the islands in the Caroline archipelago and nearest to the continent of Asia. In the centuries when maritime trade existed between India and the Mediterranean, Greek ships might have been swept off course, or possibly even explored up into Micronesia. They dropped anchor off the coast of Yap. Because of bad weather, or for other reasons, they were forced to cut their anchor cables for a hasty departure.

The lighter-skinned Europeans with their gleaming metal weapons, woven dyed clothes, and elaborately constructed ships appeared as supermen, possibly gods of the sea, to the primitive islanders. When the natives retrieved a stone anchor from the sea bottom, it was a relic of almost religious significance. The anchor was beyond price and in time became a symbol of value. Over many generations, with the memory of its origin lost, duplications of the round, flat, pierced stone actually assumed the role of currency, although in a most unwieldy form.

chapter

16

An old Grecian fable relates: A tortoise envied a frog because frogs can jump around so easily and rapidly. The turtle ceased to complain, however, when he saw frogs become the prey of a hungry eel.

Once again there is a possibly tenuous connection between the Mediterranean and the distant islands of Micronesia. Not that either turtles or eels are uncommon; they are found around the world. What is uncommon is their use in religious practices. I have looked around earlier for other sources of the sacred-turtle cult that existed in Nan Madol, and have tried to find similar words, or words in common, that might give me a lead. I realize that this can be a treacherous search, because, to determine a real linguistic correlation entire classes of words have to be considered—parts of the body, colors, animals, food, elements, et cetera.

It is not impossible, though, for a tongue to absorb an occasional foreign word into its vocabulary. Our own English language is an excellent example; we steal a word without hesitation, be it Eskimo or Hungarian. All this indicates is that at some time contact existed between the two languages and there was a need for the borrowed word. Thousands of Americans go to Tijuana, Mexico, each year to watch *jai alai*. *Jai alai* is a Basque game somewhat similar to handball, but with certain marked differences. No name existed for it in English or Spanish, so the Basque name was adopted. No one is attempting to prove a connection between the Basque and English or Spanish languages.

With this understanding, then, I have two interesting linguistic examples to consider. *Chau* was an ancient Ponapean word that denoted (1) the sun and (2) a king. The importance of this word, if any, is that it identifies the king with the sun—a concept going back to the ancient Egyptians.

A more striking example is the Polynesian word *Ra*. Ra was a sun god in their mythology. Ra was also the same word and god in Egypt and Babylonia.

So far as can be discovered, neither the Ponapeans nor the Polynesians had a written language. The sounds of the Polynesian tongue have become more or less familiar to us because of our close association with Hawaii and Tahiti, especially through their music and dancing.

Ponapean, however, strikes a Westerner's ear as completely strange and foreign. This is also true of the other tongues in Micronesia. Ponapean has been adapted into our Roman alphabet and can now be expressed in the printed word. Here is an example taken from the Ponape Almanac:

PONAPEAN	TRANSLATION
Pohnpei iei ehu wehi wenou me wiahda hahns apwen kohwahn likilik en dekehn Pacific kan. Mie deke ileike riau (Pohnpei oh Kusaie) oh me tikitik waluh me mie nehnam (Oroluk, Pakin, Ant, Mokil, Pingelap, Ngatik, Nukuor oh Kapingamarangi) ehu rehrail (Oroluk) sohte aramas mi pewe ansou wet.	Ponape is one of six districts which make up the Trust Territory of the Pacific islands. It is made up of two high islands (Ponape and Kusaie) and eight atolls (Oroluk, Pakin, Ant, Mokil, Pingelap, Ngatik, Nukuor and Kapingamarangi), one of which (Oroluk) is uninhabited now.

This example is (phonetically) the tongue spoken on the island today. What the original inhabitants spoke, probably will never be known. As we discovered earlier, linguistic experts assert that place-names are the most enduring and the last to change. Here are a few of the typical place names still found on the island:

Likiniangeir	Pohnkeimwpaiei	Imwinmap
Peikapw	Sapatir	Konterak
Peinmwiok	Nan Molusei	Nihkonok

It is difficult to recognize any similarity to a European language, so it is all the more surprising when a European-type word does appear. Not included in the above list are two other place-names that are rather startling: *Tau* and *Usen Tau*. Tau is recognizable as the nineteenth letter of the Greek alphabet, equivalent to *T*. Of course, this may be merely a coincidence; on the other hand, it may also be a holdover from a more distant age.

Again, it seems, I run into the Greeks.

Earlier I examined what is known about the religion of the Ponapeans and the inhabitants of Nan Madol. Perhaps, at this time, I should attempt to discover what theology the Greeks and the populations of Oceania might have had in common.

The religion of the Greeks has been covered in great detail by experts for many years. It is not necessary for us to go into detail here. It would seem, though, that the Greeks never attained to a uniform religious system and a fixed religious dogma. Zeus, the most powerful, ruled the Heavens; Poseidon was god of the sea; Hades was ruler of the nether world, god of the dead. All three ruled the earth. The Greek pantheon, of course, contained many more gods and goddesses—too many to enumerate here. It is interesting that Poseidon, the second-most-powerful god, was undisputed ruler of the sea.

Hades ruled the lower world of the dead. He had a kingdom of wandering spirits and ghosts. In the waters of Lethe, the souls of the dead drank forgetfulness of their earthly existence. In very early belief, Hades was not a hell in the sense of retribution for sin and evil doings. Later, however, it did punish evildoers; it also contained an abode of impenetrable darkness. Souls of the dead could be refused passage if they had not received proper burial, and if they did not pay an *obolos*. An *obolos* was a small silver coin put in the corpse's mouth for that purpose.

Originally, Elysium, blissful paradise, was located at the earth's western extremity. In later times, it was localized in the world below. Here, dead spirits, found a heaven if they did not deserve punishment in Hades.

Mt. Olympus was the home of the gods; they dwelt there. In that sense it represented Heaven. However, a few exceptions included heroes who became immortal; human souls did not achieve it.

Parallels are beginning to appear. Not too marked, perhaps, but deserving of closer scrutiny. The Ponapeans, if you recall, had three spheres of "heaven" called *Lahngs*. One was beneath the sea (don't forget the importance of the sea to Nan Madol), the second was simply the home of spirits, and the third was the home of "god." In addition, a large eternally dark pit existed for those undeserving or incompetent souls who could not cross the spinning bridge—*Kehnkepir*. Success in crossing was based on singing a song or chant. After crossing, the spirit was free to wander through all three spheres which were, apparently, blissful places.

Hades was underground and it was completely surrounded by five rivers. Originally, it was simply a place of wandering shades without memories or minds. Later, a location named Tartarus was defined in Hades to punish the wicked. Another area, Erebos, also in Hades, was eternally dark. The Elysian fields held the "good" souls and rewarded them with happiness, pleasure, and comfort.

Admittance depended on payment of an *obolos*. If friends or family forgot to include a coin in the dead man's mouth, he was eternally damned. Good or bad behavior in the deceased's lifetime had no logical bearing on the matter, any more than a soul being able to sing well enough to cross a spinning bridge in Nan Madol.

The spheres of afterlife for the Greeks were more marked

than for the Ponapeans, although they also numbered three. Hades—inhabited by shades, at peace but without memory. Tartarus where the wicked were punished. The Elysian fields, a blissful haven or heaven.

Admittedly, this comparison between Greek and Ponapean afterworlds is greatly simplified, but a slight degree of similarity does seem to exist.

The old Greeks made gods and goddesses with very human faults and frailties. I simply do not have sufficient details regarding the Ponapean deities to make a comparison, but the Polynesian gods were also very human. Often the Polynesians deified their own ancestors.

Both Polynesian and Greek religions had myths concerning incest. Among some Polynesian royal families, brothers married sisters. While this was not true of the Greeks, it was true of other Mediterranean societies, and we think of the Egyptian Pharaohs in particular.

By the fourth century B.C. many Greeks had become disillusioned with their own mythical legends and religion. The intellectuals and philosophers tried hard to rationalize their gods and goddesses. The old gods lost most of their influence, and many educated Greeks turned to philosophy. This dissension presented an opportunity for the commoners to compromise on theology and to accept more mystical theories and concepts.

We have no description of the Ponapean bridge across the eternally dark pit other than that it was a "spinning" one. Possibly it was no more than a log with treacherous footing and required perfect balancing as in log-rolling contests among lumberjacks in the American Northwest.

In early Greece, bridges were flimsy affairs of tree trunks, reeds or inflated goatskins. This primitive concept was quickly changed by Xerxes, Persian king, when he invaded Greece in 480 B.C. Xerxes bridged the Hellespont by anchoring 674 small galleys in a double line across the water. Each galley was connected by two strong cables of flax and four cables woven of papyrus. Long planks were laid across from ship to ship; brush was piled on the planks and then earth spread on the brush. A Persian army of 150,000 soldiers marched across it in safety!

(Probably the first stone bridge of record was built by the Babylonians.)

The Greeks, consequently, knew about the construction of pontoon bridges. They undoubtedly were impressed by their strength and stability—and did not forget it.

I have discussed in some detail the sailing and navigational techniques and expertise of the sailors of Polynesia and Micronesia. From very ancient times, as I found out, sea and trade routes existed between the Mediterranean, the Middle East, and India. We know, too, that the old Greeks were also expert mariners. A practical race, the Greeks early discovered that the luxuries of the Orient—spices, perfumes and incense, in particular—were in great demand and could be traded at an excellent profit.

The ancient Mediterranean sailors could sail close-hauled at an angle against the wind. Almost any ship can sail at a right angle to a strong breeze, but to sail at less than a right angle to the wind—to head *upwind*—requires a taut sail clewed almost parallel to the keel. In navigation, the angle between the keel of a close-hauled ship and the direction of the wind is measured in "points"; a point equals 11¼ degrees.

The ancient ships used the simplest possible sail—a square one—as did the Greeks. With such a sail, a well-handled ship can *sometimes* sail into the wind, but less than one point; and then, only, if the ship has a deep keel (to keep it from slipping sideways) and does not have too much of a superstructure.

Therefore, most ancient sailing was done before the wind. If the wind changed or calmed down, the sailors took to their oars.

By the fourth century B.C., Mediterranean seamen were able to clew a sail just about parallel to the keel and could sail into the wind by tacking. This required a lot of zigzag sailing and loss of time to gain a comparatively short distance upwind.

To sail a full point into the wind, a ship needs *two* masts— one at each end of the ship, or a fore-and-aft sail. The Greeks had neither the fore-and-aft sail nor a central rudder, which helps to keep a ship headed upwind; instead they used steering oars.

An Etruscan tomb painting shows a two-masted merchantman. Undoubtedly the Greeks knew about such craft, but they never adapted it. A curious incident, because the Greeks were always quick to utilize new ideas. As their trade increased, their ships became larger. Records show that Hiero II (307–216 B.C.), King of Syracuse, built a 4,000-ton ship to carry freight and passengers. This is an exception, but it does indicate to what extent Greek shipwrights were capable of building. Details regarding Hiero's big ship are missing; it would be interesting to know more about its rigging, number of oars, et cetera. Could it possibly have had a lateen sail? The old Greek sailors for centuries had sailed in Arabian waters, where the craft were so rigged and widely used. Again, it is odd that the Greeks did not adapt a lateen to their own ships.

Another interesting point to note, and perhaps another coincidence: A favorite trade item or article of barter among primitive people is the mirror. The Greeks produced beautiful metal mirrors, artistically engraved and inlaid with precious metal; these were highly prized at home. Cheaper ones could be used for trade. In Oceania, mirrors are unknown except among the Polynesians. The Polynesians had mirrors two to five inches in diameter. These circular discs were highly polished and made from fine-grained black or very dark brown basanite. The ancient Greeks were such shrewd traders, that we might conjecture that possibly the Polynesian stone mirrors were copied from original metal mirrors traded by the Greeks. After time, wear, natural deterioration, and eventual loss had destroyed the original mirrors, and because metal was not available to make new ones, the Polynesians produced their own stone imitations.

It was the *idea* that was important!

The Polynesians may have first seen the original mirrors when they moved through Micronesia, in very early days. There are no kitchen-middens or archaeological sites marking evolutionary centers in that area. Most of the islands are barren atolls with no humus to preserve important secrets of the past, so I can only guess but never be certain.

Please still bear in mind that some authorities support a theory that when the Polynesians originally moved through Micronesia, it was before the present Micronesians had arrived. The first Polynesians possibly moved in small bands held closely together and were moving under pressure. When the later bands passed through, they may have known where they were going and moved through rapidly.

This theory helps to explain why the later Micronesians had no mirrors. The original mirrors had disappeared along with the original Micronesians. The Polynesians had picked up the *idea* as they moved along; the idea was no longer there by the time the later waves of Micronesians repopulated the islands.

chapter

17

In 327 B.C., Alexander the Great, decided to invade India. Darius III, the Persian King, had been defeated in 333 B.C., but he met Alexander again and was defeated a second time in 330 B.C. Darius managed to escape with a few of his troops. At that time Alexander claimed the Persian Empire.

Now, let's go back a few years earlier to 336 B.C. In the north of China, the Hsiung-Na were causing trouble for the Chou dynasty. The emperors started building walls that eventually were completed as the Great Wall by the Ch'in dynasty over a century later. Under the Chous, people in Kansu and Shensi fled to escape work conscription and oppression. They headed to the south in small bands and kept going down the coast of Southeast Asia into Indochina.

In ancient Turkestan, about this same time, there was another problem. Today, Turkestan is part of Asia. In the days of Alexander, it was the home of the Sarmatians, a tribe of fierce fighters distinguished by their green eyes and red hair. The Sarmatians specialized in raiding caravans on the trade routes to Persia.

Alexander invaded Turkestan both in pursuit of the fleeing

Darius and to protect the trade routes to his new Persian Empire. Under heavy pressure, the Sarmatians were forced to migrate south, too, and possibly they fought their way as far as Malaysia.

Certainly, while passing through Persia, Alexander dislodged other groups as well, such as the nomadic tribes of Bactria and Sogdiana who ricocheted against other tribes in Outer Mongolia. The Mongolians, in turn, were forced against other tribes all the way to China. As a result, migrations began from Eastern Asia in 328 B.C.

From the beginning of his conquests, Alexander made it a practice to establish cities. In these new cities, the conqueror left a thin population of Greeks and Macedonians, colonies, forts and fortified posts as he went along. His armies passed through many countries besides Greece, including Asia Minor, Palestine, Egypt, Mesopotamia, Persia, Turkestan and India. The Alexandrian armies kept picking up new recruits and losing deserters.

Also, at this time, to the best of any proof, many experts believe that the islands of Polynesia were entirely unpopulated.

So it was in 327 B.C., when Alexander made his move into India. He continued in triumph to the Indus River. By now his troops were growing restless. The army had campaigned long and hard, and had been away from their homes for years. The men wanted to return.

Alexander decided to meet their wishes. He returned to the west, marching part of his army by land. The rest of his troops were to be transported to Greece by his fleet. The fleet was waiting in the Arabian Sea at the mouth of the Indus River, under the command of Admiral Nearchus. Nearchus, a friend of Alexander's, was from Crete.

The fleet under Nearchus sailed for home. But an unsubstantiated legend reports that a small number of ships did not follow the fleet, but instead turned toward the east, in the direction of the South China Sea and the Pacific. The ships that deserted varies in number up to seven and were manned by Greek officers and crewed with a mixed enlistment of Greeks, other Mediterraneans, and a large number of local Indus Valley sailors, who were, as we know, also excellent seamen.

If the deserting ships followed a course east, eventually they would pass through the Strait of Malacca into the South China Sea. Here another legend supports, to a slight degree, that such an event might have occurred. The legend relates that the ancient kingdom of Sumatra was founded by Alexander. But history documents Alexander's travels too thoroughly to support this notion.

Possibly, though, this legend might be founded on a slight and greatly distorted basis of truth. Sailing through the Strait of Malacca, the Greek ships would have to pass directly by Sumatra and may even have stopped there. Such an important event would be long remembered locally. Centuries later, the ruling royal family of Sumatra might, for matters of prestige, claim descent from such a brilliant ancestor.

Harold S. Gladwin wrote a book, *Men Out of Asia*, in 1947. He quotes from the *Cambridge Ancient History*, which says:

> Alexander greatly desired, as did Aristotle, to solve the problem of Oceania and the relationship of India to Egypt. He meant, therefore, to explore the southern sea with a fleet; for this purpose he took with him to India rowers and shipwrights from Phoenicia, Cyprus, Caria, and Egypt and had already decided that his friend, Nearchus, should be Admiral.

According to Gladwin, Alexander wanted to build a fleet of eight hundred ships. In India, Alexander began construction of this fleet including some very large ships—with three, four and five banks of oars—that carried crews of five hundred or more.

After returning from India, Alexander made Babylon his capital and concentrated on marine projects. He planned to explore the coasts of Arabia and the Indian Ocean with his new fleet. Supposedly, Nearchus reported that his fleet was ready, but before Alexander could swing into action he became ill and suddenly died in June 323 B.C.

Alexander was not quite thirty-three years old when he died. His unexpected death produced immediate chaos in Old World politics. Jealousy, greed and ambition flared among

160

Alexander's generals. His efficient political and military organization broke up.

Nearchus, admiral of the great fleet, left it to join Antigonus, a Macedonian general. Antigonus had personal plans regarding Phrygia—a country in central Asia Minor. Eventually he became King of Macedonia, Greater Phrygia, Lycia and Pamphylia. Antigonus was killed in battle in 301 B.C. For his pains, Nearchus was given the government of Lycia and Pamphylia.

After Nearchus left his command, according to Gladwin, there is no further record of the big Greek fleet, which was scattered from the mouth of the Indus to Susa, at the far-western end of the Persian Gulf.

Gladwin puts the question: What happened to all those ships? History is completely silent regarding them, although it is very explicit as to what happened to each of Alexander's generals—including Nearchus and Antigonus—and the breakup of his Empire.

A theory is proposed by Gladwin. The waiting ships had been outfitted, manned and fully supplied. He suggests that some decided to go exploring on their own; or even—as many were used to doing—began marauding the shipping around India.

And some continued to press on toward the east, past India into unknown territory. (Author's note: Although the territory to the east was unknown, it might better be described as "strange." We have seen that from very early times, mariners knew there was land in Indonesia, Malaysia, and even Micronesia. True, it was new and strange territory to the Greeks, but the Indus Valley sailors who helped man the ships must have been well aware that they were not sailing to the end of the ocean and dropping off. Sailing into a completely unknown area is different if a seaman knows there *is* land somewhere ahead, even if its exact location is vague.)

No one has an idea how many ships in Nearchus' fleet left Susa and the mouth of the Indus over the years. It is probable that most of the ships were manned by Greeks, Indus Valley sailors, and a sprinkling of other Mediterranean nationalities, but all—or almost all—were Caucasian.

In those far-off days, armies were followed by great numbers of camp followers made up of women, children, and slaves. It is not impossible that the ships carried women abroad when they pushed out on their great adventure. If they did, the women too were probably Caucasians from India.

Over the years some of the ships were wrecked and some just stopped and settled down at various points. The others, few or many, continued eastward. Many of these ships might have been quite small, *triakonters*, with no more than fifteen oars to a side.

With the help of a globe, I can try to second-guess the ships' courses as they piled their way to the South China Sea.

From the mouth of the Indus River, down the west coast of India, in a straight line, is 1,303 miles.

Around the tip of India through the Gulf of Mannar passing Sri Lanka (Ceylon), and up the east coast of India to Burma is another 1,501 miles.

Down Burma to Thailand (Siam) is an additional 711 miles.

Past Thailand through the Strait of Malacca past Sumatra is 1,422 miles.

Now the voyagers have reached the South China Sea near the foot of Malaysia. So far they have sailed 4,937 miles, reckoned in straight courses. Probably the distance actually sailed might be twice that. They did not necessarily hug the unfamiliar shore lines, because, as we have seen, it is too dangerous. But they almost certainly remained within sight of land.

Also, as established, the old Greek galleys were not equipped to store large amounts of provisions and water. So the ships, through necessity, had to stop often to replenish their stores. A custom of ships at that time, on long voyages, was to stop and sow crops. While waiting, the crews would repair and patch up their ships, and then reap the harvest.

As a ship passes through the Strait of Malacca, with Malaya on its *port*, or left, side it enters Indonesia, which includes Sumatra, Java, Borneo and Celebes. Beyond, farther to the east, is Melanesia with New Guinea and it continues as far as the Solomon Islands, the New Hebrides and Fiji.

Micronesia is to the northeast along the equator with its archipelagoes of islands—the Carolines, Marshalls and Gilberts.

Mid-Pacific is Polynesia lying in a sweeping arc with Hawaii at the north and curving down south to the Marquesas, Societies, and New Zealand.

How long did it take the Greeks to reach Indonesia after leaving the Indus? One of the reasons it is difficult to make an estimate is that there is no way of knowing how many ships might have made the journey. If a large number of ships were involved, some might have made it rather quickly by continuous sailing, stopping only at night. On the other hand, if only a comparatively few ships were involved, as seems more likely, then it might have taken a long time, even several generations or more. A number would be lost through attrition —wrecked in storms or running aground in strange waters. Others, if they were preying on shipping, might have been defeated, sunk, and taken prisoners.

Throughout their history, the Greeks maintained a reputation as colonizers. It was common practice when the mother-cities became over populated, or for political reasons, to send out bands of citizens to found a new city. It is not improbable that the crews enroute to the South China Sea, when stopping to sow crops for provisions and forced to camp for the period of a growing season, may have decided to remain at the sites of their new colonies for several years, or even many, before continuing on. New generations would have taken up the voyage at a later date to found other tiny colonies or simply to explore. So many factors have to be taken into consideration that an educated guess is impossible. But I can guess, from the legend in Sumatra, that at least *one* ship made it through the Strait of Malacca; there might have been more. We simply do not know; nor do we know even the approximate year of the event.

We cannot use the date of Alexander's death, 323 B.C., as a gauge, either. News of his death would have spread slowly to such a distant country as Sumatra. Centuries later when the legend of his fathering a dynasty there was fostered, so much time had elapsed that the date was no longer remembered and became unimportant.

On the Malabar Coast of southwest India, in Madras on the east coast, and in Burma and Siam—exactly along the route we have been tracing, the Greeks saw great dugout canoes. These canoes were very seaworthy, although they were quite primitive craft.

As the Greek ships became less seaworthy, wornout or disabled, it was easier to replace their Mediterranean vessels with native canoes than to build new triremes.

Some of the dugouts were a hundred feet long, burned and chipped out of a huge log. The Greek and Indus seamen, like sailors of all times, were skillful with their hands—jacks of all trades. When, through necessity, they were forced to take over these craft, they added nautical improvements of their own.

The sides of the great canoes were raised by adding planks to increase the freeboard. As there was no, or very little, metal ore to forge nails or fittings, the sailors sewed the planks with thin strips of bamboo and coconut fiber. They caulked the joints with leaves and pitch or resin.

In memory of the high prows of their old ships, they added high, carved posts at the bow and stern of the canoes. The new additions were carved with intricate and well-done designs. It is possible that the carvings held some religious significance and might explain the occasional use of a trident symbol found so much later among the peoples of Oceania.

The triangular lateen sails, with which the Greeks had long been familiar—from observation if not from actual use—were better adapted to the narrow canoes than the large, more unwieldy, square sails. So the lateens were added to the new craft.

Finally, do not forget that the Greeks had devised an outrigger to hold the oarlocks of their own ships. Parallel ranks of rowers, facing the stern, in such narrow craft as canoes were not practical, so they adopted the native practice of paddlers facing the bow. But they kept the idea of the outrigger and adapted it by extending it farther from one side and curving it down to the water to hold a float. The float gave the canoes, which rolled over easily, a new stability.

Sometime later, they put their knowledge of pontoon bridges into use. Remembering the stability of small boats moored side by side, back home, the Greeks substituted a second canoe for the outrigger float. The two parallel canoes were held apart, at intervals, by wood braces. By covering the braces with planks, they created a large deck for living quarters and to carry supplies. A section of the deck could be covered over, or small reed huts built on it to protect their supplies and give comfort against the elements.

Thus, the Greek and Indus immigrants created the first catamaran. This was not accomplished overnight or on the first attempt. This ultimate accomplishment resulted from a good background knowledge of sailing, a sense of adaptation, and experimentation. The big canoes could accommodate as many as thirty or more paddlers to a side; this suggests the rows of oars in a trireme. The broad deck space could hold scores of passengers and small livestock, which was more than the old Greek galleys could do.

The seaworthiness of these great catamarans was proved, later, by the Polynesians who sailed vast distances over the open Pacific. The boats are among the most seaworthy known to man, and it is doubtful that they resulted from trial-and-error methods among primitive tribesmen. Another interesting point to note is that the great canoes continued to use a long steering oar, or a long paddle, such as the Greeks used. Rudders were unknown, or at least never used, by the Polynesians or other people of Oceania. A possible exception is Micronesia.

If, as some experts believe, the Polynesians were a proto-Caucasian stock who intermarried with other Oceanic stocks, how could a very small Caucasian minority, such as the Greeks and their companions, maintain their own racial characteristics? That they did, at least for a long time, is reflected in many legends found in both Polynesia and Micronesia. According to Thor Heyerdahl, learned men of the Polynesian triangle agreed that "an industrious people with reddish hair and fair skin," claiming descent from the sun god, were found on the various islands and were expelled or absorbed by the newcomers (Polynesians). The same writer explains that an old native on Fatu Hiva, in the Marquesas, told him that the Polynesian god Tane "was white, with blond hair, and the *hao'é*, fair people like us, descended from him." It is reported this same explanation was given to E. S. C. Handy, of the B. P. Bishop Museum, in 1920.

165

Certain peoples take pride in their own stock and purposely refrain from intermarriage. Two examples in Europe are the Jews and the nomadic Gypsies. It is not improbable that the crews of Greeks and their companions remained closely knit bands; this does not rule out intermarriage with other occasional small Caucasian groups of immigrants fleeing from central Asia, such as the Sarmatians and others.

chapter
18

By 300 B.C., twenty-three years, or almost one generation, after the death of Alexander, it can be assumed that one or more of the exploring Greek crews had reached Indonesia. Each group may have kept to itself, or combined with others to establish settlements. This can explain the 2,000-year-old metal lance points found in Java.

At about that time history reveals that other peoples were migrating down the coast of China and through central Asia. These population movements put pressure on the original inhabitants as well as the newcomers. Constant raids and warfare forced the Grecian groups to continually move eastward. They moved through the Java Sea, into the Flores Sea, and then began working north through the Banda Sea. I assume that they sailed north from the Banda Sea; otherwise, by sailing south, they would have run straight into Australia.

Continuing north through the Banda Sea they reached the Molucca Passage and then sailed into the Pacific. From this point they were approximately six hundred miles away from the westernmost island of the Carolines, Palau. Yap is not far distant—slightly northeast of Palau. (Palau with its story boards, and Yap with its stone money.)

Progress from the Strait of Malacca to the Molucca Passage was slow. Very slow. The crews stopped often for provisions. When they found a suitable location, they may have established a colony and lived in it for years, or possibly several generations, before being forced to move on by another wave of migrants. Attrition—through war, disease, and especially infection—kept the Greek bands down. But there were births, too, to replace the fallen and the dead.

At least by the beginning of the Christian era, they were in Micronesia. From sources in Palau or Yap, the Greeks learned that there were scores, even hundreds, of small islands to the east. They were searching for an island, fertile and well watered, where they could settle permanently.

Almost due east from Palau in a straight line through a host of small islands and atolls lies Ponape. When the Greeks first sighted this small, magnificent island, they knew that their odyssey was over. Plants grew in abundance, with freshwater lakes and falls, and jungle growths of hard-fibered wood.

Ponape, of course, was already occupied by a small black people, but this gave no pause to the Greeks. Primitive people have no chance against more modern war equipment. The Greeks still carried some of their armor and weapons, and given this advantage, the small well-equipped band quickly overcame the original Ponapeans. Possibly, the very nature of the blacks' tribal society, with its small and mutually hostile communities, made it impossible for a great number of Ponapeans to unite against the invading Greeks.

Or, as the Incas and Aztecs in the Americas first welcomed the white-skinned Spaniards as "gods," so, possibly, the aboriginal black Ponapeans welcomed the light-skinned Greeks and Indians. Perhaps a few of the original Greek galleys still survived, but the catamarans impressed the Ponapeans equally much. The Greeks brought bows and arrows, slings and stones, very long spears and swords. Because there were no animals on the island, the blacks had no need for bows and arrows, or slings and stones. They fished and snared birds and had no need for such weapons. It is probable, though, that they did have short spears as weapons.

The blacks were easily conquered and enslaved. The Greeks, at home, practiced slavery. They soon built a society dependent on black labor. Agriculture thrived. Fruits, coconut, breadfruit, banana and plantain, tuberous plants—taro, yam, arrowroot, turmeric, and sweet potatoes—grew quickly and well. Botanists state that all these plants originated in the Indo-Malayan region, and some, if not all, the Greeks brought with them. It is not unlikely that they also brought jungle fowls (ancestors of chickens), pigs and dogs as well. Eventually, these animals became the only source of meat, except for fish, and the bounty of the sea was endless.

The tightly knit, small society of white conquerors lived easily and well.

Now, let me start counting the years. The rule of the old Saudeleurs included sixteen rulers; the length of each reign is not known. If we calculate that each was for the length of one generation, or twenty-five years, the longer ones will more or less average out with the shorter ones to an acceptable mean. On this basis, the dynasty of Saudeleurs lasted for four hundred years. Accepting the oral history that the Nahnmwarkis overthrew the last Saudeleur and immediately began a reign in a succession of twenty-one kings, and using the same average, this line of rulers continued for 525 years.

The two dynasties together ruled for a total of 925 years. Counting back from 1950, we reach a date of 1025 A.D.; this is approximate. The rulers in both dynasties were Micronesians —dark-skinned, of mixed blood. We should also remember that the Smithsonian carbon-14 date of the residue in the turtle ovens on Nan Madol, is around 1285 A.D. This does not mean that Nan Madol was *built* in 1285, or approximately, but merely that the ovens were in operation at that time. In our count back to 1025 A.D., the beginning of the Saudeleurs, this 1285 date would substantiate our theory that Nan Madol had long been built and occupied. In this instance, for 260 years.

However, there is no evidence to indicate that the Saudeleurs built the city.

If the Greeks landed on Ponape and took possession of the island around the beginning of the Christian era, there are one thousand years to account for; that is, to a time before the appearance of the Saudeleurs. This is far more than enough time for the rise and fall of any society, country or empire.

The original exploring Greeks knew something about engineering, and this knowledge was passed down to their descendants. Also, they were sailors, but *not* artists. They had the skill to raise great masses of stone into a city, but they had no desire to decorate it.

From earliest times, the Greeks, in the Mediterranean, had been seafarers. The sea was part of their tradition. In their new home, and during the generations of wandering before finding it, the tradition of the sea continued. If, as some authorities believe, Nan Madol was the center of a great, but long-forgotten, maritime empire, it was in keeping with the Greek tradition. The sea walls protecting the sea-oriented city, found nowhere else in Oceania, long had been built by the Greeks to protect their home ports against the sea and invasion. The ones at Nan Madol should come as no surprise.

The oldest legends of Ponape relate that the city was built by a black people. I believe that it was, indeed, built by the labor of the black aboriginals on the island—but they were forced to build it as slaves or conscripts under the domination of their conquerors. There is no way of knowing the population of the blacks when the Greeks and their Indus companions arrived. Or, for that matter, it is not known how many the invaders numbered either. But it can be assumed that the whites were sufficient to maintain control, and the blacks outnumbered them to the degree that they supported both themselves and their conquerors.

Several, or many, generations may have passed from the time of the first Greek occupation of the island to the beginning construction of the city. The bones reported found buried deep on the islet of Pehi en Kitel, in Nan Madol, were larger than those of later Micronesians, and certainly far larger than those of the "small black dwarfs." Because of physical limitations, the small blacks took longer on their task than did the Egyptians and Chinese in their constructions. However, there was time—plenty of it. One by one, the stone "logs" were quarried and transported to the site of the city. One by one, the islets were built and the great enclosures were erected on them. The blacks were helped in their labors by engineering devices already known to the Greeks. However, it took a long time, even a number of generations, but we will never know definitely.

During this time, the white population probably continued stable. The blacks may have decreased. Eventually, the situation became untenable for the slaves.

The Greeks brought their own religion with them to Ponape, as did their fellow Mediterranean mariners and the Indians. The ancient Greeks, at home, had always willingly and easily adopted other religious beliefs into their own. To promote unity among their companions, they did it again. Of the final beliefs and rituals one can only hazard a guess, but in one way or another they included a sacrifice of the sacred turtles —possibly from India, and an odd mixture of belief in a hereafter.

It is not too surprising that no writing of the period has been discovered. Unless written on baked tablets, which the Greeks never practiced, or engraved in stone or metal, samples could not have survived the time and elements. It is probable that the original Greek officers of the deserting ships were able to read and write. Among the ordinary crew members, it is questionable. Once the ships had started on their long journey, the need to write lessened. To whom would they write? About what? Reports to commanding officers were no longer necessary. Even supply lists could be eliminated. By the time the descendants reached Ponape, it was almost a forgotten art. A vague memory may still have remained, but the alphabet itself had disappeared with the exception of a few crude, and by now distorted characters. The "idea" of writing had been handed down, and this was important. The remnants of the Greek characters combined with ancient recollections of the Indus, plus added pictographs of their own devising, resulted in forms similar to rongo-rongo. And these were written down on boards to preserve religious chants—as were the ones on Easter Island.

Time took a toll of the Greek weapons and fittings. Some wore out, some were lost, and the rest of them simply deteriorated and rusted away. As they were lost, they were replaced by wooden copies of the originals. The Greeks made new, all-wooden bows and arrows. (Smaller versions were adopted by the blacks to hunt birds.) Nan Madol warriors developed forms of wooden armor of the kind later used by the Polynesians. They clung to their extra-long spears, now tipped with bamboo or bone; their wooden swords edged with sharks teeth or sharp stones; their spear-throwers translated from leather into wood; their shields, and their wicker-woven helmets.

Some authorities believe that the Polynesian migrations into the Pacific began around 400 A.D. Others place it later, at around 700 A.D. During that spread of three hundred years, disaster of some kind fell on Nan Madol.

Geologists say that there is no evidence of a serious earthquake striking Ponape then or recently—not one, at least, of a magnitude to level the city and make the island uninhabitable.

An epidemic might have swept the city, but if that had occurred, more bones and artifacts of the inhabitants should have been found. (The Greeks, however, did cremate their dead.) No legends of folklore support such a theory. The only decimating epidemic of which we know took place in the early part of the nineteenth century, long after Nan Madol was already a forgotten city.

A third theory is strictly my own. There are authorities who believe that construction was never entirely completed on the city. Evidence exists that work was left unfinished. After centuries of domination and slavery, the blacks revolted. Not in open warfare, because they were no match for the Greeks, but simply by running away—deserting the island. They took to their boats and sailed off searching for other islands, where they would be free of oppression. They may already have known that other blacks occupied the islands as far east as Hawaii; or, possibly, they and their descendants were the ones who reached these islands before the Polynesians.

Not all the blacks may have migrated. A few may have

retreated into the swampy jungle depths or high into the mountains. Living a guerrilla way of life, they became the fact behind the Micronesian legend of the "evil black dwarfs." With them they carried into hiding the memories of the weapons and religion of Nan Madol.

For all practical purposes, the Greeks were alone, deserted in their great city—without the labor necessary to support it. The Greeks disdained physical labor. Possibly, their maritime city had specialized in interisland trade; they no longer had trade goods gathered or raised by the blacks. The blacks had a long tradition of pearl diving. The agricultural economy of the island was gone, too, unless the Greeks wanted to replace the black labor by their own.

The city was abandoned.

Gathering up all their possessions, the migrants stripped the city of their effects and took to their great catamarans. Their numbers were not large, a few thousand or so, and they probably did not leave in a single group. A few boats at a time pushed out to sail toward the east. But, eventually, the great city was empty. And the insatiable jungle began to take over.

The emigrants from Nan Madol also knew, from their trading, that many other islands lay toward the sun. Some ships became lost and never reached a haven; others sank in storms at sea. Some, however, reached land, and these perhaps account for the old Polynesian legends of finding white inhabitants already settled on distant islands. These isolated groups were absorbed by the Polynesians, who also inherited some of the ideas, articles and customs of the refugees from Nan Madol. This would explain the similarity of dress and a degree of knowledge between the Polynesians and the Greek wanderers. Theoretically, a Polynesian king might have inherited the rongo-rongo boards and, preserved by his family, carried them eventually to Easter Island.

When the Micronesians swarmed up into Micronesia, before the Polynesian migration, but after the Greeks had started theirs, the Micronesians, too, landed on Ponape. They found a huge deserted stone city for which they could find no explanation. They took it over to their own glorification. Probably through some slight contact with the surviving black people in the mountains, they learned that the blacks had built it. The new Ponapeans may also have heard vague interpretations of the "religion" practiced by the inhabitants of the city and adapted and altered it to their own use; most surely it was an improvement, as the Ponapeans admittedly had no religion of their own at the time. Too, they discovered bows and arrows, slings, armor, and the oversized spears of the former conquerors. The few surviving blacks remained elusive in the mountains, although occasionally raiding the Ponapeans, and earned the reputation of the "evil black dwarfs." In time they assumed almost a supernatural status.

chapter
19

If the descendants of the ancient Greeks did oversee construction of Nan Madol, we should have little doubt that they knew and used engineering principles employed in their homeland. Cyclopean cities built thousands of years before had developed techniques including earthen ramps, levers, and rollers. Other more difficult problems faced the builders of Nan Madol, specifically, erecting high walls on restricted islet areas where the angles of the required ramps would be too steep to be practical. But, with the use of mechanical devices not available to much earlier primitive builders, the engineers of Nan Madol were able to overcome the problems they faced.

The Egyptians could multiply power only by increasing the number of men used, but this soon became unwieldy. They had no device for multiplication of power, as the true pulley was unknown to them. They used a "fixed" pulley that consisted of an elevated wooden beam, anchored at both ends, over which oiled cables were used for hoists. Sometimes a block of stone was used in the same manner, and such an instrument, with a groove chiseled in it for the rope to run through, has been found near the pyramids. Unfortunately, this device was not too efficient, as the friction of the rope over the beam or stone was almost as great as the force exerted.

Most experts believe that the only lifting devices known to the Egyptians were the lever, the cylindrical roller, and an extremely crude jack. It is believed that they compensated for their lack of tools by a thorough knowledge of the laws of equilibrium. Once the center of gravity of a heavy stone object was in balance at a 45-degree angle, a simple law of physics permitted it to be raised by simple human muscle power.

An Assyrian relief of the eighth century B.C. shows a representation of a true pulley. This was long after the pyramids were built and well before the time of Alexander. The first use of a pulley may have been to draw water from a deep well—a daily task. Along with the pulley was the development of the windlass employed by miners to hoist ore up a mine shaft. The crank was a natural development of the windlass. At the time of our engineers' building of Nan Madol, these mechanical devices were known and used.

The invention of two pulleys working together vastly increasing the lifting power is often attributed to Archimedes (287?–212 B.C.). This development, however, was after the time of Alexander and therefore unavailable to the builders of Nan Madol.

The wedge was widely used by all the ancient peoples. They became expert in its use for a variety of purposes. First, before metal was used, or when metal was not available, it served as a chisel, hatchet, ax, and so on. Later it was employed to split large stones and placed beneath heavy loads to help raise them.

The last device that the Greeks were heir to was the bow drill, used for drilling holes in wood, stone, and even metal, for which they had devised a way by the fourth century B.C.

Thus, we see that the ancient Greek engineers had a heritage of very simple machinery. Although their devices were unsophisticated, they were of basic significance. Later, of course, the Greeks did invent and develop clever and complex mechanical instruments.

The point is, though, that the Greeks had command of enough technology to overcome the obstacles faced in building Nan Madol, something that the primitive peoples of Oceania did not have.

A perplexing question that may never be entirely answered is why the city was built on artificial islets connected by canals. Two answers come to mind. Because the city covered a large area including considerable distances and no horses or donkeys were available for riding or pulling chariots and carts, small boats and canoes provided a quick and comfortable means of transportation. Another reason was defense. Invaders splashing their way afoot or in small craft were at a great disadvantage from the defenders of Nan Madol standing on the islets above them raining down missiles. If the foes did gain foothold on an islet, the defenders could retreat to the high walls erected on it and still maintain an advantage.

The great sea walls and the formidable barrier reef were sufficient protection against a direct attack by a flotilla. Even if a fleet came through or over the reef, the water fronting the city was too shallow to float even a large seagoing canoe.

From the clues for which I have searched, it is not unreasonable to present the theory that descendants of the Greeks of Alexander's fleet, together with Indus and Mediterranean companions, built the city of Nan Madol sometime after the beginning of the Christian era. They were able to command sufficient labor; enough food was easily available to supply the squads of workers; and there was sufficient time. In addition, the mechanical labor devices the Greeks could use overcame many of the difficulties they might have faced.

The slave labor was small, black aborigines who, when they deserted the island, took with them a knowledge of building in stone to account for other small stone constructions attributed to them throughout Polynesia. This also accounts for the Ponapean legend attributing the building of the city to a black race.

Sometime between 400 A.D., and 700 A.D., the inhabitants of

177

Nan Madol emigrated from the city. They, too, may be the early white settlers reported in the east before the Polynesians arrived. The early Polynesian migrations picked up ideas and customs tracing back to the Greeks.

When the first Micronesians settled on Ponape, sometime after 700 A.D., they found the great city deserted and took it over for their own. From reports of the few remaining blacks on the island, the Micronesians inherited some of the remembered Greek culture; possibly parts of a religion, weapons, and improved boats. But this was so distant in the past that no folk memory exists of it in Micronesia. The Ponapeans began their oral history starting with the first Saudeleur, around 1000 A.D.

Many readers will disagree with this theory. Perhaps, by now, you have reached conclusions of your own. It is almost a certainty that archaeologists, historians and other experts will disagree entirely, in part, and with each other. When this happens, possibly new research will be done on Nan Madol and more convincing evidence found.

In the opening of this book, I explained that I had long wanted to write about Nan Madol. Now that it is completed, I can report that it was *fun*—something that I thoroughly enjoyed. I hope that you have enjoyed reading it, too. I also hope that you have gathered a little information about the world of Oceania, where land is an exception in a world of sky and water.

Ko gub ni du war gag—"I have come to ask," an expression often used in Micronesia. Well, I asked. Now I will leave.

epilogue

Nothing quite like Nan Madol exists anywhere else on earth. The ancient city's construction, architecture and location are unique. The island of Ponape is only one of the "United States Trust Territory of the Pacific Islands." The Trust Territory includes 2,141 islands in a total water area equal to the continental United States, but its land mass is only half that of Rhode Island.

This great forgotten city lies in a world of its own—a land of brooding cloud-capped mountains, towering cliffs, mangrove swamps, greenhouse vegetation, tangled, unkempt jungles, and the frothy lace of breakers rolling against barrier reefs.

The United States Department of the Interior, National Park Service, has included it under the National Historic Preservation Act of 1966, as well it should.

But that is not enough!

Typhoons, time and nature have damaged the city's magnificence almost beyond belief. Each day of each passing year, the prying roots of great trees split the awesome walls only a tiny part of an inch farther asunder. The huge massive

179

stone logs fall, break, splinter and topple into the silt-filled canals. The ruins become more ruined each year.

The ruins of Nan Madol are a monument to all men—everywhere. They stand as a tribute to black, brown and white, alike—to eighty generations of our forebears who dreamed, then labored to produce something beyond dreams. This is a heritage going far past national boundaries; it belongs to all civilization. Nan Madol belongs to the world.

Occasionally in the past, scientific expeditions have cleared parts, small areas, for their investigations. When the scientists depart, the jungle immediately takes over again. Within a few months all traces of their efforts have disappeared.

Travelers into Oceania who might wish to visit the ancient ruins will find the going difficult. Access roads should be made available. None exist now. Once at the site, exploration is both disappointing and laborious. Vegetation, vines and slick moss overgrow the rocks, and footing is precarious. The thick tangle of underbrush and trees block out vision beyond a narrow perimeter. The shallow canals are so filled with silt that complete access through the winding channels to all the islets is impossible. The canals should be cleaned out so that transportation by shallow-bottom boats or canoes, as was probably intended by the original inhabitants, is easy and available.

The ruins, themselves, should be restored where restoration is possible or feasible. And the entire city area should be cleared and *kept* cleared of the jungle encroachment.

This, of course, will take money.

How much? In our national budget of astronomical billions, it would take a computer to determine the infinitesimal percentage point past the decimal. The Ponapeans, too, are proud of the ancient city. In their tight island economy, a restoration project would offer jobs and income they do not have at present. Continuing efforts of preservation would greatly help their economic development. And this would indeed be a "foreign" grant that, for once at least, would be richly returned in gratification.

It is claimed that in Palau, fishermen about once a year catch sight of a *dugong*, an increasingly rare sea mammal. The dugong, or sea cow, is thought to be the basis of the mermaid myth once so beloved by sailors everywhere. She is a most ugly animal. But whatever her actual, or claimed, charms, the dugong is now protected by law.

Nan Madol, too, is protected as a historical monument, against vandalism, defacing, destruction and theft. This is not enough! We cannot pass laws, or enforce them, against time and nature. The centuries are running out for the ancient city, but it is not too late—if we act soon.

I, for one, hope that some day my grandchildren will be able to visit and see this wonderful and almost forgotten ancient city. It is part of their right and heritage, as citizens of this world, to make the pilgrimage.

bibliography

Area Handbook for Oceania. Washington, D.C.: U.S. Government, 1971.

Berger, C. G., *Our Phallic Heritage.* New York: Greenwich Book Pubs., 1966.

Bone, Robert G., *Ancient History.* Ames, IA: Littlefield, Adams & Co., 1957.

Borden, Charles A., *South Sea Islands.* Philadelphia: MacRae Smith, 1961.

Buck, Peter H., *Vikings of the Pacific.* Chicago: Univ. of Chicago Press, 1972.

Burnstall, Aubrey F., *History of Mechanical Engineering.* Cambridge, MA.: M.I.T. Press, 1965.

Chadwick, John, *The Decipherment of Linear B.* Cambridge, England: Cambridge Univ. Press, 1958.

Childe, Gordon, *What Happened in History.* Baltimore: Penguin Books, 1965.

Christian, F. W., *The Caroline Islands.* London: Methuen, 1899.

Cirlot, J. E., *A Dictionary of Symbols.* London: Routledge & Kegan Paul, 1962.

Cleatro, P. E., *Lost Languages.* New York: John Day, 1959.

Coon, Carlton S., and James M. Andrews IV, eds., *Studies in the Anthropology of Oceania and Asia.* Cambridge, MA.: Cambridge Museum, 1943.

182

Cooper, Gordon, *Dead Cities and Forgotten Tribes*. New York: Philosophical Library, 1952.

Cornell, James, ed., *It Happened Last Year: Earth Events 1973*. New York: Macmillan Publishing Co., 1974.

Cottrell, Leonard, *The Past: A Concise Encyclopedia of Archeology*. New York: Hawthorn Books, 1960.

Daniel, Dr. Glyn, *The Idea of Prehistory*. Baltimore: Penguin Books, 1962.

——, *The Megalith Builders of Western Europe*. Baltimore: Penguin Books, 1962.

De Camp, L. Sprague, *The Ancient Engineers*. Garden City: Doubleday, 1960.

——, *Lost Continents*. New York: Dover, 1970.

De Gubernatis, Angelo, *Zoological Mythology*. London: Trübner, 1872.

Diolé, Philippe, *4,000 Years Under the Sea*. New York: Julian Messner, 1966.

Dumas, Maurice, *A History of Technology and Invention: Progress Through the Ages*. New York: Crown, 1962.

Emory, Kenneth P., "The Coming of the Polynesians," *National Geographic*, December 1974.

Forlong, J. G. R., *Encyclopedia of Religions*. New Hyde Park, N.Y.: University Books, 1964.

Gladwin, Harold Sterling, *Men Out of Asia*. New York: McGraw-Hill, 1947.

Hastings, James, *Encyclopedia of Religion and Ethics*. New York: Scribner's, 1962.

Hawkes, Jacquetta, *The First Great Civilizations*. New York: Knopf, 1973.

Heyerdahl, Thor, *Aku-Aku*. Chicago: Rand, McNally, 1958.

——, *American Indians in the Pacific*. Chicago: Rand, McNally, 1953.

——, *Fatu-Hiva*. New York: New American Library, 1974.

——, *Kon-Tiki*. Chicago: Rand, McNally, 1951.

Hibben, Dr. Frank C., *The Lost American*. New York: Crowell, 1946.

183

Jencks, Carol, *Nan Madol*. Ponape: Trust Territory of the Pacific, 1970.

Kahn, E. J., Jr., A *Reporter in Micronesia*. New York: Norton, 1965–66.
Kessing, Felix M., *Native Peoples of the Pacific World*. New York: Macmillan, 1945.

Mendelssohn, Kurt, *The Riddle of the Pyramids*. New York: Praeger, 1974.
Mertz, Henrietta, *Pale Ink*. Chicago: Swallow Press, 1953.
Montagu, Ashley, *Man: His First Million Years*. New York: New American Library, 1957.

Neuberger, Albert, *Technical Arts and Sciences of the Ancients*. New York: Barnes & Noble, 1930.

Pei, Mario, *The Story of Language*. New York: New American Library, 1949.
Ponape Almanac. Ponape: Instruct. Services Center, 1972.
Price, Willard, *America's Paradise Lost*. New York: John Day, 1966.
———, *Japan's Islands of Mystery*. New York: John Day, 1944.

Renfrew, Colin, *Before Civilization*. New York: Knopf, 1974.
Riesenberg, Saul H., *The Native Polity of Ponape*. Washington, D.C.: Smithsonian Inst. Press, 1968.
Ronan, Colin, *Lost Discoveries*. New York: McGraw-Hill, 1973.

Scott, Geoffrey, *The Architecture of Humanism*. Garden City: Doubleday, 1954.
Seyffert, Oscar, *Dictionary of Classical Antiquities*. New York: Meridian Books, 1957.
Stein, Sir Aurel, *On Alexander's Track in the Indus*. New York: Benjamin Blom, Inc., 1972.
Suggs, Robert C., *The Hidden Worlds of Polynesia*. New York: Harcourt, Brace & World, 1962.

Taylor, Prof. E. G. R., *The Haven-Finding Art*. New York: Abelard-Schuman, 1957.

Thiel, Rudolph, *And There Was Light*. New York: New American Library, 1960.

Trumbull, Robert, *Paradise in Trust*. New York: Sloane, 1959.

Valentine, Tom, *The Great Pyramid*. New York: Pinnacle Books, 1975.

Vincent, James M., ed., *Micronesia's Yesterday*. Saipan, Mariana Is.: Trust Territory of the Pacific, Dept. of Education, 1973.

Weckler, J. E., *Polynesians: Explorers of the Pacific*. Darby, Pa.: Darby Books, reprint of a 1943 edition.

index

Caroline Islands, 13, 20, 60; canoes in, 119; lack of metal, 108; languages, 140; maps, 14, 17; rongo-rongo in, 135, 136

Caroline Islands, The (Christian), 114–15

Catamarans, 120; and abandonment of Nan Madol, 173; theories on, 165; *see also* Canoes

Caucasians, in Micronesia, Polynesia, 165

Chau, origin of word, 151

Chaucer, Geoffrey, 126

China, Chinese: ancient navigation, 74; Ch'in dynasty, 158; compass, 128; cotton in, 107; Great Wall, 23, 73–74, 158; and Indonesia, 108–09; language characteristics, 74–75; and North America, 71–73; population movements, 167; possible links with Micronesians, Polynesians, 70–71, 99, 100; use of compass, 128; writing materials, 137

Ch'in dynasty, 158

Chokalai, 114, 116

Chou dynasty, 73, 158

Christian, F. W., 29, 114–15, 116

Churchill, William, 130

Churchward, James, and Mu, 57

Classic of Mountains and Seas (*Shan Kai King*), 71–72

Compass, origin of, 127–28

Cottrell, Leonard, 136

Counting systems: 137–38, 139; *see also* Stone "money"

Cousteau, Jacques, 54–55

Crete, 54, 79, 80; bull worship, 82; conch war trumpet, 117; Linear A, B, 81, 138; Phaistos Disc, 138; seafaring, 143–44

Cultures and inventions, 49–50

Cyclopean walls: Greece, 144; Micronesia, 104–05

Daniel, Glyn, 49, 50

Darius I (the Great), 127, 146

Darius III, 158, 159

Darong (site), 32, 34

Dawson, Dr. Mary R., 55

Die Osterinselschrift (Heine-Geldern), 134

Diffusionists, 49, 50, 96

Diolé, Philippe, 89, 149

Dionysios the Elder, 145–46

Dowas Pah (site), 36

Dowas Powe (site), 36

Dravidians, 81

Dugongs (sea cows), 180–81

Durkheim, Émile, 142

Eagle, two-headed, 128–29

Earth, geology of, 58–59

Earthquakes: and abandonment of cities, 69–70; and topographical changes, 59

Easter Island, 20, 41, 56, 106, 171; carbon-dating on, 100; and Mu-Lemuria theories, 56, 57; rongo-rongo, 81–82, 131–32, 133, 134–35; stone heads, 94, 103–04

Eels, sacred, 31–32, 67; *see also* Turtle cults

Egypt (ancient): architectural devices, 84–85; and Atlantis, 53; building, engineering, 87–88, 127, 145, 175–76; conservatism, 136; mummy wrappings, 107; pyramids (*see* Great Pyramid); seamanship, 124; turtle symbols, 66; writing materials, 137

Elysium, 153, 154

Emory, Dr. Kenneth P., 106, 121, 123

Ethnological Museum, Hamburg, 40

Ethnology of Polynesia and Micronesia (Linton), 115

Euphrates Valley, floods in, 52

Europe–North America land bridge, 55–56

Evans, Sir Arthur, 138

Evolutionists, 49, 50

Falcon (British ship), 47

Faraulep Island, counting system, 137, 139

Fatu Hiva, Marquesas, 103

Fiji Islands, 20; and Mu-Lemuria, 56, 57; and Polynesians, 100

Folklore, defined, 43

Geophysical report (1973) on earthquakes, 59

Gilbert Islands, 20, 105

Gilgamesh (Babylonian god), 129

Gladwin, Harold, 160, 161

Gorgias (Greek sophist), 52

Great Bath, Mohenjo Daro, 78

Great Pyramid of Khufu (Cheops), 23, 76, 84–87